Rise
Above
Crisis

Rise Above Crisis

James Allen

MEDIA

Published 2020 by Gildan Media LLC
aka G&D Media
www.GandDmedia.com

Front Cover design by David Rheinhardt of Pyrographx

Interior design by Meghan Day Healey of Story Horse, LLC

Library of Congress Cataloging-in-Publication Data is available upon request

ISBN: 978-1-7225-0352-9

10   9   8   7   6   5   4   3   2   1

Contents

Light
on Life's
Difficulties

I, Truth, am thy Redeemer, come to Me;
    Lay down thy sin and pain and wild unrest;
And I will calm thy spirit's stormy sea,
    Pouring the oil of peace upon thy breast:
Friendless and lone—lo, I abide with thee.

Defeated and deserted, cast away,
    What refuge hast thou? Whither canst thou fly?
Upon my changeless breast thy burdens lay;
    I am thy certain refuge, even I:
All things are passing; I alone can stay.

Lo I, the Great Forsaken, am the Friend
    Of the forsaken; I, whom men despise,
The weak, the helpless, and despised defend;
    I gladden aching hearts and weeping eyes;
Rest thou in Me, I am thy sorrow's end.

Lovers and friends and wealth, pleasures and fame—
    These fail and change, and pass into decay;
But My Love does not change; and in thy blame
    I blame thee not, nor turn my face away:
In My calm bosom hide thy sin and shame.

Contents

Foreword

When a man enters a dark room he is not sure of his movements; he cannot see the objects around, or properly locate them, and is liable to hurt himself by coming into sudden contact with them; but let a light be introduced, and immediately all confusion disappears, every object is seen, and there is no more danger of being hurt.

To the majority life is such a dark room, and their frequent hurts—their disappointments, perplexities, sorrows, and pains—are caused by sudden contact with principles which they do not see, and are therefore not prepared to deal with; but when the light of wisdom is introduced into the darkened understanding, confusion vanishes, difficulties are dissolved, all things are seen in their true place and proportion, and henceforth the man walks, open-eyed and unhurt, in the clear light of a wise comprehension.

—James Allen
Bryngoleu,
Ilfracombe, England

The Light That Leads to Perfect Peace

This book is intended to be a strong and kindly companion, as well as a source of spiritual renewal and inspiration to those who aim at a life well-lived and made strong and serene. It will help its readers to transform themselves into the ideal character thy would wish to be, and to make their life here that blessed thing which the majority only hope for in some future life.

Our life is what we make it by our own thoughts and deeds. It is our own state and attitude of mind which determine whether we are happy or unhappy, strong or weak, sinful or holy, foolish or wise. If one is unhappy, that state of mind belongs to himself, and is originated within himself; it is a state which responds to certain outward happenings, but its *cause* lies within, and not in those outward occurrences. If one is weak in will, he has brought himself to, and remains in, that condition by the course of thought and action which he has chosen and is still choosing. If one is sinful, it is because he has committed, and continues to commit, sinful acts. If he is foolish, it is because he himself does foolish things.

A man has no character, no soul, no life apart from his thoughts and deeds. What they are, that he is. As they are modified, so does he change. He is endowed with will, and can modify his character. As the carpenter changes the block of wood into a beautiful piece of furniture, so can the erring and sin-stricken man change himself into a wise and truth-loving being.

Each man is responsible for the thoughts which he thinks and the acts which he does, for his state of mind, and the life which he lives. No power, no event, no circumstance can compel a man to evil and unhappiness. He himself is his own compeller. He thinks and acts by his own volition. No being, however wise and great—not even the Supreme— can make him good and happy. He himself must choose the good, and thereby find the happy.

And because of this—*that when a man wishes and wills* he can find the Good and the True, and enjoy its bliss and peace—there is eternal gladness in the Courts of Truth, and holy joy amongst the Perfect Ones.

The Gates of Heaven are forever open, and no one is prevented from entering by any will or power but his own; but no one can enter the Kingdom of Heaven so long as he is enamored of, and chooses, the seductions of hell, so long as he resigns himself to sin and sorrow.

There is a larger, higher, nobler, diviner life than that of sinning and suffering, which is so common—in which, indeed, nearly all are immersed—a life of victory over sin, and triumph over evil; a life wise and happy, benign and tranquil, virtuous and peaceful. This life can be found and lived now, and he who lives it is steadfast in the midst of change; restful among the restless; peaceful, though surrounded by strife. Should death confront him, he is calm; though assailed by persecution, he knows no bitterness, and his heart is compassionate and filled with rejoicing. In this supremely beautiful life there is no evil, sin and sorrow are ended, and aching hearts and weeping eyes are no more.

This life of triumph is not for those who are satisfied with any lower conditions; it is for those who thirst of it and are willing to achieve it; who are as eager for righteousness as the miser is for gold. It is always at hand, and is offered to all, and blessed are they who accept and embrace it; they will enter the World of Truth; they will find the Perfect Peace.

Light on Facts and Hypotheses

When freedom of thought and freedom of expression abound, there is much controversy and much confusion, yet it is from such controversial confusion that the simple facts of life emerge, attracting us with their eternal uniformity and harmony, and appealing forcibly to us with their invisible simplicity and truth.

We are living in such an age of freedom and mental conflict. Never were religious sects so numerous. Schools—philosophical, occult, and otherwise—abound, and each is eager for the perpetuation and dominance of its own explanation of the universe. The world is in a condition of mental ferment. Contradiction has reached the point of confusion, so that the earnest seeker for Truth can find no solid rock of refuge in the opposing systems which are presented to him, and is thereby thrown back upon himself, upon those incontrovertible facts of his own being which are ever with him—which are, indeed, himself, his life.

Controversy is ranged around hypotheses, not around facts. Fact is fixed and final; hypothesis is variable and vanishing. In his present stage of development, man is not alive to the beautiful simplicity of facts, nor to the power of satisfaction which is inherent in them; he does not perceive the intrinsic loveliness of truth, but must add something to it; hence, when a fact is named, the question almost invariably arises, "How can you explain the fact?" and then follows a hypothesis which leads to another hypothesis, and so on and on until the fact is altogether lost sight of amid a mass of contradictory suppositions. Thus arise the sects and controversial schools.

The clear perception of one fact will lead to the perception of other facts, but a supposition, while appearing to elucidate a fact, does in reality cover it up. We cannot realize the stately splendor of Truth while playing with the gaudy and attractive toys of pretty hypotheses. Truth is not an opinion, nor can any opinion enlarge or adorn it. Fact and supposition are eternally separate, and the cleverest intellectual jugglery—while it may entertain and deceive even the elect—cannot in the slightest degree alter a fact or affect the nature of things-as-they-are. Because of this, the true teacher abandons the devious path of hypothesis, and deals only with the simple facts of life, fixing the attention of men upon these, instead of increasing confusion and intensifying wordy warfare by foisting another assumption upon a world already lost and bewildered in a maze of hypotheses.

The facts of life are ever before us, and can be understood and known if we but abandon our egotism and the blinding delusions which that egotism creates. Man need not go beyond his own being to find wisdom, and the facts of that being afford a sufficient basis on which to erect a temple of knowledge of such beauty and dimensions that it shall at once emancipate and glorify.

Man is; and as he thinks, so he is. A perception and realization of these two facts alone—of man's being and thinking—lead into a vast avenue of knowledge which cannot stop short of the highest wisdom and perfection. One of the reasons why men do not become wise is that they occupy themselves with interminable speculations about a *soul* separate from themselves—that is, from their own mind—and so blind themselves to their actual nature and being. The supposition of a separate soul veils the eyes of man so that he does not see himself, does not know his mentality, is unaware of the nature of his thoughts without which he would have no conscious life.

Man's life is actual; his thoughts are actual; his life is actual. To occupy ourselves with the investigation of things that are, is the way of wisdom. Man considered as above, beyond, and separate from mind and thought, is speculative and not actual, and to occupy ourselves with the study of things that are not, is the way of folly.

Man cannot be separated from his mind; his life cannot be separated from his thoughts. Mind, thought, and life are as inseparable as light, radiance, and color, and are no more in need of another factor to elucidate them than are light, radiance, and color. The facts are all-sufficient, and contain within themselves the groundwork of all knowledge concerning them.

Man as mind is subject to change. He is not something "made" and finally complete, but has within him the capacity for progress. By the universal law of evolution he has *become* what he is, and is becoming that which he will be. His being is modified by every thought he thinks. Every experience affects his character. Every effort he makes changes his mentality. Herein is the secret of man's degradation, and also of his power and salvation if he but utilize this law of change in the right choice of thought.

To live is to think and act, and to think and act is to change. While man is ignorant of the nature of thought, he continues to change for better or worse; but, being acquainted with the nature of thought, he intelligently accelerates and directs the process of change, and only for the better.

What the sum total of a man's thoughts are, that he is. From the sameness of thought with man there is not the slightest fractional deviation. There is a change of result with the addition and subtraction of thought, but the mathematical law is an invariable quantity.

Seeing that man is mind, that mind is composed of thought, and that thought is subject to change, it follows the deliberately to change the thought is to change the man.

All religions work upon the heart, the thought of man, with the object of directing it into purer and higher channels; and success in this direction, whether partial or complete, is called "salvation"— that is, deliverance from one kind of thought, one condition of mind, by the substitution of another thought, another condition. It is true that the dispensers of religion today do not know this because of the hypothetical veil which intervenes between the fact and their consciousness; but they *do* it without knowing it, and the Great Teachers who founded the various religions, built upon this fact, as their precepts plainly show. The chief things upon which these Teachers lay such stress, and so constantly reiterate—such as the purification of the heart, the thinking of right thoughts, and the doing of good deeds—what are they but calls to a higher, nobler mode of thought-energizing forces urging men to effort in the choosing of thoughts which shall lift them into realms of greater power, greater good, greater bliss?

Aspiration, meditation, devotion—these are the chief means which men in all ages employ to reach up to higher modes of thought, wide airs of peace, vaster realms of knowledge, for "as he thinketh in his heart, so is he"; he is saved from himself—from his own folly and suffering—by creating within new habits of thoughts, by becoming a new thinker, a new man.

Should a man by a supreme effort succeed in thinking as Jesus thought—not by imitation, but by a sudden realization of his indwelling power— he would be as Jesus. In the Buddhistic records there is an instance of a man, not the possessor of great piety or wisdom, who asked Buddha how one might attain the highest wisdom and enlightenment, and Buddha replied, "by ceasing from all desire"; and it is recorded that the man let go all personal desires and at once realized the highest wisdom and enlightenment. One of the sayings of Buddha runs, "The only miracle with which a wise man concerns himself is the transformation of a sinner into a saint," and Emerson referred to this transforming power of change of thought when he said:

"It is as easy to be great as to be small,"

which is closely akin to that other great and oft-repeated but little understood saying:

"Be ye therefore perfect, even as your Father which is in Heaven is perfect."

And, after all, what is the fundamental difference between a great man and a small one? It is one of thought, of mental attitude. True, it is one of knowledge, but then, knowledge cannot be separated from thought; and every substitution of a better for a worse thought is a transforming agency which marks an important advance in knowledge. Throughout the whole range of human life, from the lowest savage to the highest type of man, thought determines character, condition, knowledge.

The mass of humanity moves slowly along the evolutionary path urged by the blind impulse of its dominant thoughts as they are stimulated and called forth by external things; but the true thinker, the sage, travels swiftly and intelligently along a chosen path of his own. The multitudes, unenlightened concerning their spiritual nature, are the slaves of thought, but the sage is the master of thought. They follow blindly; he chooses intelligently. They obey the impulse of the moment, thinking of their immediate pleasure and happiness; he commands and subdues impulse, resting upon that which is permanently right. They, obeying blind impulse, violate the law of righteousness; he, conquering impulse, obeys the law of righteous. The sage stands face to face with the facts of life. He knows the nature of thought. He understands and obeys the law of his being.

But the sorrow-burdened victim of blind impulse can open his mental eyes and see the true nature of things when he wishes to do so. The sage— intelligent, radiant, calm—and the fool—confused, darkened, disturbed—are one in essence, and are divided only by the nature of their thoughts; when the fool turns away from and abandons his foolish thoughts and chooses and adopts wise thoughts, lo! he becomes a sage.

Socrates saw the essential oneness of virtue and knowledge, and so every sage sees. Learning may aid and accompany wisdom, but it does not lead to it. Only the choosing of wise thoughts, and necessarily, the doing of wise deeds, leads to wisdom. A man may be learned in the schools, but foolish in the school of life. Not the committing of words to memory, but the establishing oneself in purer thoughts, nobler thinking, leads to the peace-giving revelations of true knowledge.

Folly and wisdom, ignorance and enlightenment, are not merely the result of thought, they are thought itself. Both cause and effect—effort and result—are contained in thought.

> *All that we are is the result of what we have*
> *thought.*
> *It is founded on our thoughts; it is made up of*
> *our thoughts.*

Man is not a being possessing a soul, another self. He himself is soul. He himself is the thinker and doer, actor and knower. His composite mentality is himself. His spiritual nature is rounded by his sphere of thought. He it is that desires and sorrows, enjoys and suffers, loves and hates. The mind is not the instrument of a metaphysical, superhuman soul. Mind is soul; mind is being; mind is men.

Man can find himself. He can see himself as he is. When he is prepared to turn from the illusory and self-created world of hypothesis in which he wanders, and to stand face to face with actuality, then will be known himself as he is; moreover, he can picture himself as he would wish to be and can create within him the new thinker, the new man; for every moment is the time of choice—and every hour is destiny.

Light on the Law of Cause and Effect in Human Life

How frequently people associate the word "law" with hardness and cruelty! It seems to embody, for them, nothing but an inflexible tyranny. This arises partly from their inability to perceive principles apart from persons, and partly from the idea that the office of law is solely to punish. Viewed from such an attitude of mind, the term *law* is hazily regarded as some sort of indefinite personality whose business it is to hunt transgressors and crush them with overwhelming punishments.

Now while law punishes, its primary office is to *protect*. Even the laws which man makes, are framed by him to protect himself from his own baser passions. The law of our country is instituted for the protection of life and property, and it only comes into operation as a punishing factor when it is violated. Offenders against it probably think of it as cruel, and doubtless regard it with terror, but to them that obey it, it is an abiding protector and friend, and can hold for them no terror.

So with the Divine Law which is the stay of the Universe, the heart and life of the Cosmos—it is that which protects and upholds, and it is no less protective in its penalties than in its peaceful blessings; it is, indeed, an eternal protection which is never for one moment withheld, and it shields all beings against themselves by bringing all violations of itself, whether ignorant or willful, through pain to nothingness.

Law cannot be partial. It is an unvarying mode of action, disobeying which, we are hurt; obeying, we are made happy. Neither protestation nor supplication can alter it, for if it could be altered or annulled the universe would collapse and chaos would prevail.

It is not less kind that we should suffer the penalty of our wrong-doing than that we should enjoy the blessedness of our right-doing. If we could escape the effects of our ignorance and sin, all security would be gone, and there would be no refuge, for we could then be equally doubtful of the result of our wisdom and goodness. Such a scheme would be one of caprice and cruelty, whereas law is a method of justice and kindness.

Indeed, the supreme law is the principle of eternal kindness, faultless in working, and Infinite in application. It is none other than that.

Eternal Love, forever full,
Forever flowing free.

of which the Christian sings; and the "Boundless Compassion" of Buddhistic precepts and poetry. The law which punishes us is the law which preserves us. When in their ignorance men would destroy themselves, its everlasting arms are thrown about them in loving, albeit sometimes painful, protection. Every pain we suffer brings us nearer to the knowledge of the Divine Wisdom. Every blessing we enjoy speaks to us of the perfection of the Great Law, and of the fulness of bliss that shall be man's when he has come to his heritage of Divine Knowledge. We progress by learning, and we learn, up to a certain point, by suffering. When the heart is mellowed by love, the law of love is perceived in all its wonderful kindness; when wisdom is acquired, peace is assured.

We cannot alter the law of things, which is of sublime perfection, but we can alter ourselves so as to comprehend more and more of that perfection, and make its grandeur ours. To wish to bring down the perfect to the imperfect is the height of folly, but to strive to bring the imperfect up to the perfect is the height of wisdom.

Seers of the Cosmos do not mourn over the scheme of things. They see the universe as a perfect whole, and not as an imperfect jumble of parts. The Great Teachers are men of abiding joy and heavenly peace.

The blind captive of unholy desire may cry:

Ah! Love; could you and I with him conspire
To grasp this sorry scheme of things entire.
Would we not shatter it to bits, and then
Remould it nearer to the heart's desire?

This is the wish of the voluptuary, the wish to enjoy unlawful pleasures to any extent, and not reap any painful consequences. It is such men who regard the universe as a "sorry scheme of things."

They want the universe to bend to their will and desire; want lawlessness, not law; but the wise man bends his will and subjects his desires to the Divine Order, and he sees the universe as the glorious perfection of an infinitude of parts.

Buddha always referred to the moral law of the universe as the Good Law, and indeed it is not rightly perceived if it is thought of as anything but good; for in it there can be no grain of evil, no element of unkindness. It is no iron-hearted monster crushing the weak and destroying the ignorant, but a soothing love and brooding compassion shielding the tenderest from harm, and protecting the strongest from a too destructive use of their strength. It destroys all evil, it preserves all good. It enfolds the tiniest seedling in its care, and it destroys the most colossal wrong with a breath. To perceive it, is the beatific vision; to know it, is the beatific bliss; and they who perceive and know it are at peace; they are glad forever more.

Such is the law which moves to righteousness,
Which none at last can turn aside or stay;
The heart of it is love; the end of it
Is peace and consummation sweet: obey.

Light on Values—
Spiritual and
Material

It is an old-time axiom that "everything has its price." Everybody knows this commercially, but how few know it spiritually. Business consists of a mutual interchange of equitable values. The customer gives money and receives goods, and the merchant gives goods and receives money. This method is universal, and is regarded by all as just. In spiritual things the method is the same, but the form of interchange is different. For material things a material thing is given in exchange, but for spiritual things a spiritual thing is given in exchange. Now these two forms of exchange cannot be transposed; they are of reverse natures, and remain eternally separate. Thus a man may take a sovercign to a shop and ask for a pound's worth of food, or clothing, or literature, and he will receive goods to the value of his sovereign; but if he were to take a sovereign to a teacher of Truth, and ask to be supplied with a pound's worth of religion, or righteousness, or wisdom, he would be told that those things cannot be purchased with money, that their spiritual nature excludes them from material business transactions. The wise teacher, however, would also tell him that these spiritual necessities *must* be purchased, that though money cannot buy them, yet they have their price, that something must be parted with before they can be received, that, in a word, instead of offering money he must offer up self, or selfishness. For so much selfishness given up, so much religion, righteousness, and wisdom would be immediately received, and this without fail, and with perfect equity, for if a man is sure of receiving perishable material food and clothing for the money he puts down, how much more surely will he receive the imperishable spiritual sustenance and protection for the selfishness which he lays down! Shall the law operate in the lesser, and fail in the greater? Man may fail to observe the law, but the law is infallible.

A man may love his money, but he must part with it before he can receive the material comforts of life. Likewise a man may love his selfish gratifications, but he must give them up before he can receive the spiritual comforts of religion.

Now when a tradesman gives goods for money, it is not that he may keep the money, but that he may give it in exchange for other goods. The primary function of business is not to enable everybody to hoard up money, but to facilitate the interchange of commodities. The miser is the greatest of all failures, and he may die of starvation and exposure while being a millionaire, because he is a worshipper of the letter of money, and an ignorer of its spirit—the spirit of mutual interchange. Money is a means, not an end; its exchange is a sign that goods are being justly given and received. Thus commerce, with all its innumerable ramifications of detail, is reducible to one primary principle, namely:

Mutual interchange of the material necessities of life.

Now let us follow this principle into the spiritual sphere, and trace there its operation. When a religious man gives spiritual things—kindness, sympathy, love—and receives happiness in return, it is not that he may hoard and hug to himself that happiness, but that he may give it to others, and so receive back spiritual things. The primary function of religion is not to enable all to hoard up personal pleasure, but to render actual the interchange of spiritual blessings. The most selfish man—he whose chief object is the getting of happiness for himself—is a spiritual miser, and his mind may perish of spiritual destitution though he be surrounded with the objects which he has obtained to pander to his pleasure, because he is worshipping the letter of happiness, and is ignoring its spirit—the spirit of unselfish interchange. The object of selfishness is the getting of personal pleasure, or happiness; the object of religion is the diffusion of virtue. Thus religion, with all its innumerable creeds, may be resolved into one primary principle, namely:

Mutual interchange of spiritual blessings.

What, then, are the spiritual blessings? They are kindness, brotherliness, goodwill, sympathy, forbearance, patience, trustfulness, peacefulness, love unending, and compassion unlimited. These blessings, these necessities for the starving spirit of man, can be obtained, but their price *must* be paid; unkindness, uncharitableness, ill-will, hardness, ill-temper, impatience, suspicion, strife, hatred, and cruelty—all these, along with the happiness, the personal satisfaction, which they give must be yielded up. These spiritual coins, dead in themselves, must be parted with, and when parted with, there will be immediately received their spiritual counterparts, the living and imperishable blessings to which they are a means and of which they are a sign.

To conclude, when a man gives money to a merchant, and receives goods in return, he does not wish to have his money again. He has willingly parted with it forever, and is satisfied with the exchange. So when a man gives up unrighteousness in exchange for righteousness, he does not wish to have his selfish pleasures back again. He has given them up forever, and is satisfied and in peace.

Thus also, when one bestows a gift, even though it be a material gift, he does not look for the receiver to send him back its value in money, because it is a religious deed, and not a business transaction. The material thing thus given represents the interchange of a spiritual blessing, and its accompanying bliss, the bliss of a gift bestowed, and that of a gift received.

"Are not two sparrows sold for a farthing?" Everything in the universe—every object and every thought—is valued. Material things have a material value, spiritual things have a spiritual value, and to confound these values is not wise. To seek to purchase spiritual blessings with money, or material luxuries with virtue, is the way of selfishness and folly. It is to confound barter with religion, and to make a religion of barter. Sympathy, kindness, love cannot be bought and sold, they can only be given and received. When a gift is paid for, it ceases to be a gift.

Because everything has a value, that which is freely given is gained with accumulation. He who gives up the lesser happiness of selfishness, gains the greater happiness of unselfishness. The universe is just, and its justice is so perfect that he who has once perceived it can no more doubt or be afraid, he can only wonder and be glad.

Light on
the Sense
of Proportion

In a nightmare there is no relation of one thing to another; all things are haphazard, and there is general confusion and misery. Wise men have likened the self-seeking life to a nightmare; and there is a close resemblance between a selfish life, in which the sense of proportion is so far lost that things are only seen as they affect one's own selfish aims, and in which there are feverish excitements and overwhelming troubles and disasters, and that state of troubled sleep known as nightmare.

In a nightmare, too, the controlling will and perceiving intelligence are asleep; and in a selfish life the better nature and spiritual perceptions are locked in profound slumber.

The uncultivated mind lacks the sense of proportion. It does not see the right relation of one natural object to another, and is therefore dead to the beauty and harmony with which it is surrounded.

And what is this sense of proportion but the faculty of *seeing things as they are!* It is a faculty which needs cultivating, and its cultivation, when applied to natural objects, embraces the entire intelligence and refines the moral nature. It enters, however, into spiritual things as well as things natural, and here is more lacking, and more greatly needed; for to see things as they are in the spiritual sphere, is to find no ground for grief, no lodging place for lamentation.

Whence spring all this grief and anxiety, and fear and trouble? Is it not because things are not as men wish them to be? Is it not because the multiplicity of desires prevents them from seeing things in their true perspective and right proportion?

When one is overwhelmed with grief, he sees nothing but his loss, its nearness to him blots out the whole view of life. The thing in itself may be small, but to the sufferer it assumes a magnitude which is out of all proportion to the surrounding objects of life.

All who have passed the age of thirty, can look back over their lives at times when they were perplexed with anxiety, overwhelmed with grief, or even, perhaps, on the verge of despair, over incidents which, seen now in their right proportion, are known to be very small.

If the would-be suicide will today stay his hand, and wait, he will at the end of ten years marvel at his folly over so comparatively small a matter.

When the mind is possessed by passion or paralyzed with grief, it has lost the power of judgment, it cannot weigh and consider, it does not perceive the relative values and proportions of the things by which it is disturbed; awake and acting, it yet moves in a nightmare which holds its faculties in thrall.

The passionate partisan lacks this sense of proportion to such an extent, that to him his own side or view appears all that is right and good, and his opponent's all that is bad and wrong. To this partiality his reason is chained, so that whatever reason he may bring to bear upon the matter, is enlisted in the service of bias, and is not exercised in order to find the just relation which exists between the two sides. He is so convinced that his own party is all right, and the other, equally intelligent, party is all wrong, that it is impossible for him to be impartial and just. The only thing he understands as justice is that of getting his own way, or placing some ruling power in the hands of his party.

Just as the sense of proportion in things material puts an end to the spirit of repugnance, so in things spiritual it puts an end to the spirit of strife. The true artist does not see ugliness anywhere, he sees only beauty. That which is loathsome to others, fills, to him, its rightful place in nature, and it appears in his picture as a thing of beauty. The true seer does not see evil anywhere, he sees universal good. That which is hateful to others, he sees in its rightful place in the scheme of evolution, and it is held dispassionately in his mind as an object of contemplation.

Men worry, and grieve, and fight, because they lack this sense of proportion, because they do not see things in their right relations. The objects of their turbulence are not things-in-themselves, but their own opinions about things, self-created shadows, the unreal creations of an egoistic nightmare.

The cultivation and development of the ethical sense of proportion converts the heated partisan into the gentle peacemaker, and gives the calm and searching eye of the prophet to the hitherto blind instrument in the clashing play of selfish forces.

The spiritual sense of proportion gives sanity; it restores the mind to calmness; it bestows impartiality and justice, and reveals a universe of faultless harmony.

Light on Adherence to Principle

The man of Truth never departs from the divine principles which he has espoused. He may be threatened with sickness, poverty, pain, loss of friends and position, yea, even with immediate death, yet he does not desert the principles which he knows to be eternally true. To him, there is one thing more grievous, more to be feared and shunned than all the above evils put together, and that is—*the desertion of principle*. To turn coward in the hour of trial, to deny conscience, to join the rabble of passions, desires, and fears, in turning upon, accusing, and crucifying the Eternal Christ

of Divine Principle, because, forsooth, that principle has not given him personal health, affluence
and ease—this, to the man of Truth, is the evil of
evils, the sin of sins.

We cannot escape sickness and death. Though
we avoid them for a long time, in the end they will
overtake us. But we can escape wrong-doing, we
can avoid fear and cowardice; and when we eschew
wrong-doing and cast out fear, the evils of life will
not subdue us when they overtake us, for we shall
have mastered them; instead of avoiding them for
a season we shall have conquered them on their
own ground.

There are those who teach that it is right to do
wrong when that wrong is to protect another; that
it is good, for instance, to tell a lie when its object
is the well-being of another—that is, that it is right
to desert the principle of truthfulness under severe
trial. Such teaching has never emanated from the
lips of the Great Teachers. It has not been uttered
even by those lesser, yet superbly noble men, the
prophets, saints, and martyrs, for these divinely
illuminated men knew full well that no circumstance can make a wrong a right, and that a lie has
no saving and protective power. Wrong-doing is a
greater evil than pain, and a lie is more deadly and
destructive than death. Jesus rebuked Peter for trying to shield his Master's life by wrong-doing, and

no right-minded person would accept life at the expense of the moral character of another when it appeared possible to do so.

All men admire and revere the martyrs, those steadfast men and women who feared wrong, cowardice, and lying, but who did not fear pain and death; who were steadfast and calm in their adherence to principle even when brought to the utmost extremity of trial, yea, even when the taunts and jeers of enemies assailed them, and the tears and agonies of loved ones appealed to them, they flinched not nor turned back, knowing that the future good and salvation of the whole world depended upon their firmness in that supreme hour; and for this, they stand through all time as monuments of virtue, centres of saving and uplifting power for all humankind. But he who lied to save himself, or for the sake of the two or three beings whom he personally loved, is rarely heard of, for in that hour of desertion of principle, his power was gone; and if he *is* heard of, he is not loved for that lie; he is always looked upon as one who fell when the test was applied; as an example of the highest virtue he is rejected by all men in all times.

Had all men believed that an untruth was right under extreme circumstances, we should have had no martyrs and saints, the moral fibre of humanity would have been undermined, and the world left to grope in ever deepening darkness.

The attitude which regards wrong-doing for the sake of others as the right thing to do, is based on the tacit assumption that wrong and untruth are inferior evils to unhappiness, pain, and death; but the man of moral insight knows that wrong and untruth are the greater evils, and so he never commits them, even though his own life or the lives of others appear to be at stake.

It is easy for a man in the flowery time of ease or the heyday of prosperity to persuade himself that he is staunchly adhering to principle, but when pain overtakes him, when the darkness of misfortune begins to settle down upon him, and the pressure of circumstances hems him in—then he is on his trial, then he has come to his testing time; in that season it will be brought to the light whether he clings to self or adheres to Truth.

Principles are for our salvation in the hour of need. If we desert them in that hour, how can we be saved from the snares and pains of self?

If a man does wrong to his conscience, thinking thereby to avoid some immediate pain or pressing evil, he does but increase pain and evil. The good man is less anxious to avoid pain than wrong-doing.

There is neither wisdom nor safety in deserting permanent and protective principles when our happiness seems to be at stake. If we desert the true for the pleasant, we shall lose both the pleasant and the true; but if we desert the pleasant for the true, the peace of truth will soothe away our sorrow. If we barter the higher for the lower, emptiness and anguish will overtake us, and then, having abandoned the Eternal, where is our rock of refuge? But if we yield up the lower for the higher, the strength and satisfaction of the higher will remain with us, fulness of joy will overtake us, and we shall find in truth a rock of refuge from the evils and sorrows of life.

To find the permanent amid all the changes of life, and, having found it, adhere to it under all circumstances—this only is true happiness, this only is salvation and lasting peace.

Light on the Sacrifice of the Self

elf-sacrifice is one of the fundamental principles in the teaching of all the Great Spiritual Masters. It consists in yielding up self, or selfishness, so that Truth may become the source of conduct. Self is not an entity that has to be cast out, but a condition of mind that has to be converted. The renunciation of self is not the annihilation of intelligent being, but the annihilation of every dark and selfish desire. Self is the blind clinging to perishable things and transient pleasures as distinguished from the intelligent practice of virtue and righteousness. Self is the lusting, coveting, desiring of the heart, and it is this that must be yielded up before Truth can be known, with its abiding calm and endless peace.

To give up *things* will not avail; *it is the lust for things* that must be sacrificed. Though a man sacrifice wealth, position, friends, fame, home, wife, child—yea, and life also—it will not avail if self is not renounced. Buddha renounced the world and all that it held dear to him, but for six years he wandered and searched and suffered, and not till he yielded up the desires of his heart did he become enlightened and arrive at peace.

By giving up only the *objects* of self-indulgence, no peace will ensue, but torment will follow. It is self-indulgence, *the desire for the object*, that must be abandoned—then peace enters the heart.

Sacrifice is painful so long as there is any vestige of self remaining in the heart. While there remains in the heart a lurking desire for an unworthy object or pleasure that has been sacrificed, there will be periods of intense suffering, and fierce temptation; but when the *desire* for the unworthy object or pleasure is put away forever from the mind, and the sacrifice is complete and perfect, then, concerning that particular object or pleasure, there can be no more suffering or temptation. So when self in its entirety is sacrificed, sacrifice, in its painful aspect, is at an end, and perfect knowledge and perfect peace are reached.

Hatred is self; covetousness is self; envy and jealousy are self; malice is self; pride and superciliousness are self; vanity and boasting are self; gluttony and sensuality are self; lying and deception are self; speaking evil of one's neighbor is self; anger and revenge are self. Self-sacrifice consists in yielding up all these dark conditions of mind and heart. The process is a painful one in its early stages, but soon a divine peace descends at intervals upon the pilgrim; later, this peace remains longer with him, and finally, when the rays of Truth begin to be shed abroad in the heart, remains with him.

This sacrifice leads to peace; for in the perfect life of Truth, there is no more sacrifice, and no more pain and sorrow; for where there is no more self there is nothing to be given up; where there is no clinging of the mind to perishable things there is nothing to be renounced; where all has been laid upon the altar of Truth, selfish love is swallowed up in divine love; and in divine love there is no thought of self, for there is the perfection of insight, enlightenment, and immortality, and therefore perfect peace.

Light on the Management of the Mind

ollowing the last chapter a few hints on the management of one's mind will doubtless be opportune. Before a man can see even the necessity for thorough and complete self-government, he will have to throw off a great delusion in which so many are involved—the delusion of believing that his lapses of conduct are due to those about him, and not entirely to himself. "I could make far greater progress if I were not hindered by others," or "It is impossible for me to make any headway, seeing that I live with such irritable people," are commonly expressed complaints which spring from the error of imagining that others are responsible for one's own folly.

The violent or irritable man always blames those about him for his fits of anger, and by continually living in this delusion, he becomes more and more confirmed in his rashness and perturbations, for how can a man overcome—nay, how can he even try to overcome, his weakness if he convinces himself that it springs entirely from the actions of others? Moreover, firmly believing this, as he does, he vents his anger more and more upon others in order to try and make matters better for himself, and so becomes completely lost to all knowledge of the real origin of his unhappy state.

Men cast the blame of their unprosperous acts
Upon the abettors of their own resolve,
Or anything but their weak guilty selves.

All a man's weaknesses and sins and falls take their rise in his own heart, and he alone is responsible for them. It is true there are tempters and provokers, but temptations and provocations are powerless to him who refuses to respond to them. Tempters and provokers are but foolish men, and he who gives way to them has become a willing co-operator in their folly; he is unwise and weak, and the source of his troubles is in himself. The pure man cannot be tempted; the wise man cannot be provoked.

Let a man fully realize that he is absolutely responsible for his every action, and he has already gone a considerable distance along the path which leads to wisdom and peace, for he will then commence to utilize temptation as a means of growth, and the wrong conduct of others he will regard as a test of his own strength.

Socrates thanked the gods for the gift of a shrewish wife in that it enabled him the better to cultivate the virtue of patience; and it is a simple and easily perceived truth that we can the better grow patient by living with the impatient, better grow unselfish by living with the selfish. If a man is impatient with the impatient, he is himself impatient; if he is selfish with the selfish, then he is himself selfish. The test and measure of virtue is trial, and, like gold and precious stones, the more it is tested the brighter it shines. If a man thinks he has a virtue, yet gives way when its opposing vice is presented to him, let him not delude himself, he has not yet attained to the possession of that virtue.

If a man would rise and become a man indeed, let him cease to think the weak and foolish thought, "I am hindered by others," and let him set about to discover that he is hindered only by himself; let him realize that the giving way to another is but a revelation of his own imperfection, and lo! upon him will descend the light of wisdom, and the door of peace will open unto him, and he will soon become the conqueror of self.

The fact that a man is continually troubled and disturbed by close contact with others, is an indication that he requires such contact to impel him onward to a clearer comprehension of himself, and toward a higher and more steadfast state of mind. The very things which he regards as insurmountable hindrances will become to him the most valuable aids when he fully realizes his moral responsibility and his innate power to do right. He will then cease to blame others for his unmanly conduct, and will commence to live steadfastly under all circumstances; the scales of self-delusion will quickly fall from his eyes, and he will then see that ofttimes when he imagined himself provoked by others, he himself was really the provoker; and as he rises above his own mental perturbations, the necessity for coming in contact with the same conditions in others will cease, and he will pass, by a natural process, into the company of the good and pure, and will then awaken in others the nobility which he has arrived at in himself.

> *Be noble! and the nobleness that lies*
> *In other men, sleeping, but never dead,*
> *Will rise in majesty to meet thine own.*

Light on Self-Control: The Door of Heaven

The foremost lesson which the world has to learn on its way to wisdom, is the lesson of self-control. All the bitter punishments which men undergo in the school of experience are inflicted because they have failed to learn this lesson. Apart from self-control, salvation is a meaningless word, and peace is an impossibility; for how can a man be saved from any sin whilst he continues to give way to it? or how can he realize abiding peace until he has conquered and subdued the troubles and perturbations of his mind?

Self-control is the Door of Heaven; it leads to light and peace. Without it a man is already in hell; he is lost in darkness and unrest. Men inflict upon themselves far-reaching sufferings, and pass through indescribable torments, both of body and soul, through lack of self-control; and not until they resort to its practice can their sufferings and torments pass away, for it has no substitute, nothing can take its place, and there is no power in the universe that can do for a man that which he, sooner or later, *must* do for himself, by entering upon the practice of self-control.

By self-control a man manifests his divine power and ascends toward divine wisdom and perfection. Every man can practice it. The weakest man can begin now, and until he does begin, his weakness will remain, or he will become weaker still. Calling or not calling upon God or Jesus, Brahma or Buddha, Spirits or Masters, will not avail men who refuse to govern themselves and to purify their hearts. Believing or disbelieving that Jesus is God, that Buddha is omniscient, or the Spirits or Masters guide human affairs, cannot help men who continue to cling to the elements of strife and ignorance and corruption within themselves.

What theological affirmation or denial can justify, or what outward power put right, the man who refuses to abandon a slanderous or abusive tongue, or give up an angry temper, or to sacrifice his impure imaginings? The flower reaches the upper light by first contending with the under darkness, and man can only reach the Light of Truth by striving against the darkness within himself.

The vast importance of self-control is not realized by men, its absolute necessity is not apprehended by them, and the spiritual freedom and glory to which it leads are hidden from their eyes. Because of this, men are enslaved and misery and suffering ensue. Let a man contemplate the violence, impurity, disease, and suffering which obtain upon earth, and consider how much of it is due to want of self-control, and he will gradually come to realize the great need there is for self-control.

I say again, that self-control is the Gate of Heaven, for without it neither happiness nor love nor peace can be realized and maintained. In the degree that it is lacked by a man, in just that measure will his mind and life be given over to confusion, and it is because such a large number of individuals have not yet learned to practice it that the enforced restraint of national laws is required for the maintenance of order and the prevention of a destructive confusion. Self-control is the beginning of virtue, and it leads to the acquisition of every noble attribute; it is the first essential quality in a well-ordered and truly religious life, and it leads to calmness, blessedness, and peace. Without it, although there may be theological belief or profession, there can be no true religion, for what is religion but enlightened conduct? and what is spirituality but the triumph over the unruly tendencies of the mind?

When men both depart from and refuse to practice self-control, then they fall into the great and dark delusion of separating religion from conduct; then they persuade themselves that religion consists, not in overcoming self and living blamelessly, but in holding a certain belief about Scripture, and in worshipping a certain Saviour in a particular way; hence arise the innumerable complications and confusions of letter-worship, and the violence and bitter strife into which men fall in defence of their own formulated religion. But true religion cannot be formulated; it is purity of mind, a loving heart, a soul at peace with the world. It needs not to be defended, for it is Being and Doing and Living. A man begins to practice religion when he begins to control himself.

Light on Acts and Their Consequences

One of the commonest excuses for wrong-doing is that if right were done calamity would ensue. Thus the foolish concern themselves, not with the act, but with the consequence of the act, a foreknowledge of which is assumed. The desire to secure pleasant results, and to escape unpleasant consequences, is at the root of that confusion of mind which renders men incapable of distinguishing between good and evil, and prevents them from practising the one and abandoning the other. Even when it is claimed that the wrong thing is done, not for one's self, but in order to secure the happiness of others, the delusion is the same, only it is more subtle and dangerous.

The wise concern themselves with the act, and not with its consequences. They consider, not what is pleasant or unpleasant, but *what is right*. Thus doing what is right only, and not straining after results, they are relieved of all burdens of doubt, desire, and fear. Nor can one who so acts ever become involved in an inextricable difficulty, or be troubled with painful perplexity. His course is so simple, straight, and plain that he can never be confused with misgivings and uncertainties. Those who so act are said by Krishna to act "without regard to the fruits of action," and he further declares that those who have thus renounced results are supremely good, supremely wise.

Those who work for pleasant results only, and who depart from the right path when their, or others', happiness appears to be at stake, cannot escape doubt, difficulty, perplexity, and pain. Ever forecasting probable consequences, they act in one way today, and in another way tomorrow; unstable, and blown about by the changing winds of circumstance, they become more and more bewildered, and the consequences about which they trouble do not accrue.

But they who work for righteousness only, who are careful to do the right act, putting away all selfish considerations, all thought of results, they are steadfast, unchanging, untroubled and in peace amid all vicissitudes, and the fruits of their acts are ever sweet and blessed.

Even the knowledge, which only the righteous possess, that wrong acts can never produce good results, and that right acts can never bring about bad results, is in itself fraught with sweet assurance and peace. For whether the fruits of acts are sought or unsought, they cannot be escaped.

They who sow to self, and, ignorant of the law of Truth, think they can make their own results, reap the bitter fruits of self.

They who sow to righteousness, knowing themselves to be the reapers, *and not the makers of consequences*, reap the sweet fruits of righteousness.

Right is supremely simple, and is without complexity. Error is interminably complex, and involves the mind in confusion.

To put away self and passion, and establish one's self in right-doing, this is the highest wisdom.

Light on the Way of Wisdom

The Path of Wisdom is the highest way, the way in which all doubt and uncertainty are dispelled and knowledge and surety are realized.

Amid the excitements and pleasures of the world and the surging whirlpools of human passions, Wisdom—so calm, so silent and so beautiful—is indeed difficult to find, difficult, not because of its incomprehensible complexity, but because of its unobtrusive simplicity, and because self is so blind and rash, and so jealous of its rights and pleasures.

Wisdom is "rejected of men" because it always comes right home to one's self in the form of wounding reproof, and the lower nature of man cannot bear to be reproved. Before Wisdom can be acquired, self must be wounded to the death, and because of this, because Wisdom is the enemy of self, self rises in rebellion, and will not be overcome and denied.

The foolish man is governed by his passions and personal cravings, and when about to do anything he does not ask "Is this right?" but only considers how much pleasure or personal advantage he will gain by it. He does not govern his passions and act from fixed principles, but is the slave of his inclinations and follows where they lead.

The wise man governs his passions and puts away all personal cravings. He never acts from impulse and passion, but dispassionately considers what is right to be done, and does it. He is always thoughtful and self-possessed, and guides his conduct by the loftiest moral principles. He is superior to both pleasure and pain.

Wisdom cannot be found in books or travel, in learning or philosophy, it is *acquired by practice only*. A man may read the precepts of the greatest sages continually, but if he does not purify and govern himself he will remain foolish. A man may be intimately conversant with the writings of the greatest philosophers, but so long as he continues to give way to his passions he will not attain to wisdom.

Wisdom is right action, right doing; folly is wrong action, wrong-doing. All reading, all study, all learning is vain if a man will not see his errors and give them up. Wisdom says to the vain man, "Do not praise yourself," to the proud man, "Humble yourself," to the gossip, "Govern your tongue," to the angry man, "Subdue your anger," to the resentful man, "Forgive your enemy," to the self-indulgent man, "Be temperate," to the impure man, "Purge your heart of lust," and to all men, "Beware of small faults, do your own duty faithfully, and never intermeddle with the duty of another."

These things are very simple; the doing of them is simple, but as it leads to the annihilation of self, the selfish tendencies in man object to them and rise up in revolt against them, loving their own life of turbulent excitement and feverish pleasure, and hating the calm and beautiful silence of Wisdom. Thus men remain in folly.

Nevertheless, the Way of Wisdom is always open, is always ready to receive the tread of the pilgrim who has grown weary of the thorny and intricate ways of folly. No man is prevented from becoming wise but by himself; no man can acquire Wisdom but by his own exertions; and he who is prepared to be honest with himself, to measure the depths of his ignorance, to come face to face with his errors, to recognize and acknowledge his faults, and at once to set about the task of his own regeneration, such a man will find the way of Wisdom, walking which with humble and obedient feet, he will in due time come to the sweet City of Deliverance.

Light on Disposition

I cannot help it, it is my disposition." How often one hears this expression as an excuse for wrong-doing. What does it imply? This, that the person who utters it believes that he has no choice in the matter, that he cannot alter his character. He believes that he must go on doing the wrong thing to the end of his days because he was "born so," or because his father or grandfather was like it; or, if not these, then some one along the family line a hundred, or two or three hundred years ago must have been afflicted, and therefore he is and must remain so. Such a belief should be uprooted, destroyed, and cast away, for it is not only without reason, it is a complete barrier to all progress, to all growth in goodness, to all development of character and noble expansion of life. Character is not permanent; it is, indeed, one of the most changeable things in nature. If not changed by a conscious act of the will, it is being continually modified and re-formed by the pressure of circumstances. Disposition is not fixed, except in so far as one fixes it by continuing to do the same thing, and by persistence in the stubborn belief that he "cannot help it." Immediately one gets rid of that belief he will find that he *can* help it; further, he will find that intelligence and will are instruments which can mould disposition to any extent, and that, too, with considerable rapidity if one is in earnest.

What is disposition but a habit formed by repeating the same thing over and over again? Cease repeating (doing) the thing, and lo! the disposition is changed, the character is altered. To cease from an old habit of thought or action is, I know, difficult at first, but with each added effort the difficulty decreases, and finally disappears, and then the new and good habit is formed and the disposition is changed from bad to good, the character is ennobled, the mind is delivered from torment and is lifted into joy.

There is no need for any one to remain the slave of a disposition which causes him unhappiness, and which he himself regards as undesirable. He can abandon it. He can break away from the slavery. He can deliver himself and be free.

Light on Individual Liberty

Within the sphere of his own mind man has all power, but in the sphere of other minds and outside things, his power is extremely limited. He can command his own mind, but he cannot command the mind of others. He can choose what he shall think, but he cannot choose what others shall think. He cannot control the weather as he wills, but he can control his mind, and decide what his mental attitude toward the weather shall be.

A man can reform the dominion of his own mind, but he cannot reform the outer world because that outer world is composed of other minds having the same freedom of choice as himself. A pure being cannot cleanse the heart of one less pure, but by his life of purity and by elucidating his experience in the attainment of purity, he can, as a teacher, act as a guide to others, and so enable them more readily and rapidly to purify themselves. But even then those others have all power to decide whether they shall accept or reject such guidance, so complete is man's choice.

It is because of this dual truth—that man has no power in the outer realm of others' minds and yet has all power over his own mind, that he cannot avoid the consequences of his own thoughts and acts. Man is altogether powerless to alter or avert consequences, but he is altogether powerful in his choice of causative thought. Having chosen his thoughts, he must accept their full consequences; having acted, he cannot escape the full results of his act.

Law reigns universally, and there is perfect individual liberty. A man can do as he likes, but all other men can do as they like. A man has power to steal, but others have power to protect themselves against the thief. Having sent out his thought, having acted his purpose, a man's power over that thought and purpose is at an end; the consequences are certain and cannot be escaped, and they will be of the nature of the thought and act which produced them—painful or blessed.

Seeing that a man can think and do as he chooses, and that all others have the like liberty, a man has to learn, sooner or later, to reckon with other minds, and until he does this he will be ceaselessly involved in suffering. To think and act apart from the consideration of others is both an abuse of power and an infringement of liberty. Such thoughts and acts are annulled and brought to nought by the harmonizing Principle of Liberty itself, and such annulling and bringing to nought is felt by the individual as suffering. When the mind, rising above ignorance, recognizes the magnitude of its power within its own sphere and, ceasing to antagonize itself against others, it harmonizes itself to those other minds, acknowledging their freedom of choice, then is realized spiritual plenitude and the cessation of suffering.

Selfishness, egotism, and despotism are, from the spiritual standpoint, transferable terms; they are one and the same thing. Every selfish thought or act is a manifestation of egotism, is an effort of despotism, and it is met with suffering and defeat: it is annulled because the Law of Liberty cannot, in the smallest particular, be annulled. If selfishness could conquer, Liberty would be non-existent, but selfishness fails of all results but pain, because Liberty is supreme. An act of selfishness contains two elements of egotism: namely, (1) the denial of the liberty of others, and (2) the assertion of one's own liberty beyond its legitimate sphere. It thereby destroys itself. Despotism is death.

Man is not the creature of selfishness, he is the maker of it; it is an indication of his power—his power to disobey even the law of his being. Selfishness is power without wisdom; it is energy wrongly directed. A man is selfish because he is ignorant of his nature and power as a mental being; such ignorance and selfishness entail suffering, and by repeated suffering and age-long experience he at last arrives at knowledge and the legitimate exercise of his power. The truly enlightened man cannot be selfish: he cannot accuse others of self-ishness, or try to coerce them into being unselfish.

The selfish man is eager to bend others to his own way and will, believing it to be the only right way for all; he thereby ignorantly wastes himself in trying to check in others the power which he freely exercises himself, namely—the power to choose their own way and exercise their own will. By so doing, he places himself in direct antagonism with the like tendencies and freedom of other minds, and brings into operation the instruments of his own suffering. Hence the ceaseless inter-play of conflicting forces; the unending conflagration of passion; the turmoil, strife, and woe. Selfishness is misapplied power.

The unselfish man is he who, ceasing from all personal interference, abandoning the "I" as the source of judgment, and having recognized his illimitable freedom through the abandonment of all egotism even in thought, refrains from encroachment upon the boundless freedom of others, realizing the legitimacy of their choice and their right to the free employment of their power. However others may choose to act toward such a man, it can never cause him any trouble or suffering, because he is perfectly willing that they should so choose to act, and he harbors no wish that they should act in any other way. He realizes that his sole duty, as well as his entire power, *lies in acting rightly toward them*, and that he is in no way concerned with their actions toward him; that is both their choice and their business. To the unselfish man, therefore, malice, envy, backbiting, jealousy, accusation, condemnation, and persecution have passed away. Having ceased to practice these things, he is not disturbed when they are hurled at him. Thus liberation from sin is liberation from suffering. The selfless man is free; he has made the thraldom of sin impossible; he has broken every bond.

Light on the Blessing and Dignity of Work

That "labor is life" is a principle pregnant with truth, and one which cannot be too often repeated, or too closely studied and practised. Labor is so often regarded as an irksome and even degrading means of obtaining ease and pleasure, and not as what it really is—a thing happy and noble in itself, that the lesson contained in the maxim needs to be taken to heart and more and more thoroughly learned.

Activity, both mental and physical, is the essence of life. The complete cessation of activity is death, and death is immediately followed by corruption. Ease and death are closely associated. The more there is of activity, the more abounding is life. The brain-worker, the original thinker, the man of unceasing mental activity, is the longest-lived man in the community; the agricultural laborer, the gardener, the man of unceasing physical activity, comes next with length of years.

Pure-hearted, healthy-minded people love work, and are happy in their labors. They never complain of being "overworked." It is very difficult, almost impossible, for a man to be overworked if he lives a sound and pure life. It is worry, bad habits, discontent and idleness that kill—especially idleness, for if labor is life, then idleness must be death. Let us get rid of sin before we talk about being overworked.

There are those who are afraid of work, regarding it as an enemy, and who fear a breakdown by doing too much. They have to learn what a health-bestowing friend work is. Others are ashamed of work, looking upon it as a degrading thing to be avoided. The "pure in heart and sound in head" are neither afraid nor ashamed of work, and they dignify whatsoever they undertake. No necessary work can be degrading, but if a man regard his work as such, he is already degraded, not by his task, but by his slavish vanity.

Man hath his daily work of body and mind
Appointed, which declares his dignity.

The idle man who is afraid of work, and the vain man who is ashamed of it, are both on the way to poverty, if they are not already there. The industrious man, who loves work, and the man of true dignity, who glorifies work, are both on their way to affluence, if they are not already there. The lazy man is sowing the seeds of poverty and crime; the vain man is sowing the seeds of humiliation and shame. The industrious man is sowing the seeds of affluence and virtue; the dignified worker is sowing the seeds of victory and honor. Deeds are seeds, and the harvest will appear in due season.

There is a common desire to acquire riches with as little effort as possible, which is a kind of theft. To try to obtain the fruits of labor without laboring is to take the fruits of another man's labor; to try to get money without giving its equivalent is to take that which belongs to another and not to one's self. What is theft but this frame of mind carried to its logical extreme?

Let us rejoice in our work; let us rejoice that we have the strength and capacity for work, and let us increase that strength and capacity by unremitting labor. Whatever our work may be, it is noble, and will be perceived by the world as noble, if we perform it in a noble spirit. The virtuous do not despise any labor which falls to their lot; and he who works and faints not, who is faithful, patient, and uncomplaining even in the time of poverty, he will surely at last eat of the sweet fruits of his labor; yea, even while he labors and seems to fail, happiness will be his constant companion, for, "Blessed is the man that has found his work; let him ask no other blessedness."

Light on Good Manners and Refinement

Move upward, working out the beast,
And let the ape and tiger die.

All culture is getting away from the beast. Evolution itself is a refining process, and the unwritten laws of society inhere in the evolutionary law.

Education is intellectual culture. The scholar is engaged in purifying and perfecting his intellect; the religious devotee is engaged in purifying and perfecting his heart.

When a man aspires to nobler heights of achievement, and sets about the realization of his ideal, he commences to refine his nature; and the more pure a man makes himself within, the more refined, gracious, and gentle will be his outward demeanor.

Good manners have an ethical basis, and cannot be divorced from religion. To be ill-mannered is to be imperfect, for what are ill manners but the outward expression of inward defects? What a man does, that he is. If he acts rudely, he is a rude man; if he acts foolishly, he is a foolish man; if he acts gently, he is a gentleman. It is a mistake to suppose that a man can have a gentle and refined mind behind a rough and brutal exterior (though such a man may possess some strong animal virtues), as the outer is an expression of the inner.

One of the steps in the noble Eightfold Path to perfection as expounded by Buddha is—Right Conduct or Good Behavior, and it should be plain to all that the man who has not yet learned how to conduct himself toward others in a kindly, gracious, and unselfish spirit, has not yet entered the pathway of a holy life.

If a man refines his heart, he will refine his behavior; if he refines his behavior, it will help him to refine his heart.

To be coarse, brutish, and snappish may be natural to a beast, but the man who aspires to be even an endurable member of society (not to mention the higher manhood), will at once purge away any such bestial traits that may possess him.

All those things which aid in man's refinement—such as music, painting, poetry, manners—are servants and messengers of progress. Man degrades himself when he imitates the brute. Let us not mistake barbarism for simplicity, or vulgarity for honesty.

Unselfishness, kindliness, and consideration for others will always be manifested outwardly as gentleness, graciousness, and refinement. To affect these graces by simulating them may seem to succeed, but it does not. Affectation and hypocrisy are soon divulged; every man's eye, sooner or later, pierces through their flimsiness, and ultimately none but the actors of them are deceived.

As Emerson says:

> *What is done for effect, is seen to be done for*
> *   effect; and what is done for love,*
> *is felt to be done for love.*

Children who are well-bred are taught always to consider the happiness of others before their own: to offer them the most comfortable seat, the choicest fruit, the best tidbit, and so on; and also to do everything, even the most trivial acts, in the right way. And these two things—*unselfishness and right action*—are at the basis, not only of good manners, but of all ethics, religion, and true living:

they represent power and skill. The selfish man is weak and unskilful in the exercise of thought; the vulgar man is weak and unskilful in his actions. Unselfishness is the right way of thinking; good manners are the right way of acting. As Emerson, again, says:

> *There is always a best way of doing everything,*
> *if it be to boil an egg. Manners are the happy*
> *way of doing things right.*

It is a frequent error among men to imagine that the Higher Life is an ideal something quite above and apart from the common details of life, and that to neglect these or to perform them in a slovenly manner is an indication that the mind is occupied on "higher things." Whereas it is an indication that the mind is becoming inexact, dreamy, and weak, instead of exact, wide awake, and strong. No matter how apparently trivial the thing is which has to be done, there is a right way and a wrong way of doing it, and to do it in the right way saves friction, time, and trouble, conserves power, and develops grace, skill, and happiness.

The artisan has a variety of tools with which to ply his particular craft, and he is taught (and also finds by experience) that each tool must be applied to its special use, and never under any circumstances must one tool be made to do service for another. By using every tool in its proper place and in the right way, the maximum of dexterity and power is attained. Should a boy in learning a trade refuse instruction, and persist in using the tools in his own way, making one tool do service for another, he would never become anything better than a clumsy bungler, and would be a failure in his trade.

It is the same throughout the whole life. If a man opens himself to receive instruction, and studies how to do everything rightly and lawfully, he becomes strong and skilful and wise, master of himself, his thoughts and actions; but if he persists in following his momentary impulses, in doing everything as he feels prompted, not exercising thoughtfulness, and rejecting instruction, such a man will attain to nothing better than a slovenly and bungling life.

Confucius paid the strictest attention to dress, eating, deportment, passing speech—to all the so-called trivialities of life, as well as to the momentous affairs of state and the lofty moral principles which he expounded; and he taught his disciples that it is the sign of a vulgar and foolish mind to regard anything as "trivial" that is necessary to be done, that the wise man pays attention to all his duties, and does everything wisely, thoughtfully, and rightly.

It is not an arbitrary edict of society that the man who persists in eating with his knife shall be rejected, for a knife is given to cut with, and a fork to eat with, and to put things to wrong and slovenly uses—even in the passing details of life—does not make for progress, but is retrogressive and makes for confusion.

It is not a despotic condition in the law of things that so long as a man persists in thinking and acting unkindly of and toward others he shall be shut out from Heaven, and shall remain in the outer pain and unrest, for selfishness is disruption and disorder. The universe is sustained by exactness, it rests on order, it demands right doing, and the searcher for wisdom will watch all his ways. He will think purely, speak gently, and act graciously, refining his entire nature, both in the letter and the spirit.

Light on Diversities of Creeds

Those who depart from the common track in matters of faith, and strike out independently in search of the Higher Life as distinguished from the letter of religious dogma, are apt to sink into a pitfall which awaits them at the first step, namely, the pitfall of *pride*. Attacking "creeds," and speaking contemptuously of "the orthodox" (as though orthodoxy were synonymous with evil) are not uncommon practices among those who fondly imagine they are in possession of greater spiritual light. Departure from orthodoxy does not by any means include departure from sin; indeed, it is not infrequently accompanied with increased bitterness and contempt. Change of opinion is one thing, change of heart is quite another. To withdraw one's adherence from creeds is easy; to withdraw one's self from sin is more difficult.

Hatred and pride, and not necessarily orthodoxy and conformity, are the things to be avoided. One's own sin, and not another man's creed, is the thing to be despised. The right-minded man cannot plume himself on being "*broader*" than others, or assume that he is on a "higher plane" than others, or think with pharisaical contempt of those who still cling to some form of letter worship which he has abandoned. Applying the words "narrow," "bigoted," and "selfish" to others, is not the indication of an enlightened mind. No person would wish these terms to be applied to himself, and he who is becoming truly religious, does not speak of others in words which would wound him were they directed toward himself.

Those who are learning how to exercise humility and compassion are becoming truly enlightened. Thinking lowly of themselves and kindly of others; condemning their own sins with merciless logic, and thinking with tender pity of the sins of others, they develop that insight into the nature and law of things which enables them to see the truth that is in others, and in the religions of others, and they do not condemn their neighbor because he holds a different faith, or because he adheres to a formal creed. Creeds must be, and he who performs faithfully his duty in his particular creed, not interfering with or condemning his neighbor in the performance of his duty, is bringing the world nearer to perfection and peace.

Amid all the diversities of creeds there is the unifying power of undying and unalterable Love—and he who has Love has entered into sympathetic union with all.

He who has acquired the true spirit of Religion, who has attained to pure insight and deep charity of heart, will avoid all strife and condemnation, and will not fall into the delusion of praising his own sect (should he belong to one) and trying to prove that it alone is right, and of dispraising other sects, and trying to prove that they are false. As the true man does not speak in praise of himself or his own work, so the man of humility, charity, and wisdom does not speak of his own sect as being superior to all others, nor seek to elevate his own particular religion by picking holes in forms of faith which are held as sacred by others.

Nothing more explicit and magnanimous has ever been uttered, in reference to this particular phase of the practice of charity, than is to be found in the twelfth Edict of Asoka, the great Indian

Ruler and Saint who lived some two or three centuries previous to the Christian era, and whose life, devoted to the spread of Truth, testified to the beauty of his words: the edict runs thus:

> There should be no praising of one's own sect and decrying of other sects; but, on the contrary, a rendering of honor to other sects for whatever cause honor may be due. By so doing, both one's own sect may be helped forward, and other sects will be benefited; by acting otherwise, one's own sect will be destroyed in injuring others. Whosoever exalts his own sect by decrying others, does so doubtless out of love for his own sect, thinking to spread abroad the fame thereof. But, on the contrary, he inflicts the more an injury upon his own sect.

These are wise and holy words; the breath of charity is in them, and they may be well pondered upon by those who are anxious to overthrow, not the religions of other men, but their own shortcomings.

It is a dark and deep-seated delusion that causes a man to think he can best advance the cause of his own religion by exposing what he regards as the "evils" of other religions; and the most pitiful part of it is, that while such a one rejoices in the thought that by continually belittling other sects he will perhaps at last wipe them out, and win all men to his side, he is all the time engaged in the sad work of bringing into disrepute, and thereby destroying, his own sect.

Just as every time a man slanders another, he inflicts lasting injury upon his own character and prospects, so every time one speaks evil of another sect, he soils and demeans his own. And the man who is prone to attack and condemn other religions is the one who suffers most when his own is attacked and condemned. If a man does not like that his own religion should be denounced as evil and false, he should carefully guard himself that he does not condemn other religions as such. If it pleases him when his own cause is well spoken of and helped, he should speak well of and help other causes which, while differing from his own in method, have the same good end in view. In this way he will escape the errors and miseries of sectarian strife, and will perfect himself in divine charity.

The heart that has embraced gentleness and charity avoids all those blind passions which keep the fires of party strife, violence, persecution, and bitterness burning from age to age. It dwells in thoughts of pity and tenderness, scorning nothing, despising nothing, not stirring up enmity; for he who acquires gentleness, gains that clear insight into the Great Law which cannot be obtained in any other way, he sees that there is good in all sects and religions, and he makes that good his own.

Let the truth-seeker avoid divisions and invidious distinctions, and let him strive after charity; for charity does not slander, backbite, or condemn; it does not think of trampling down another's, and elevating its own.

Truth cannot contradict itself. The nature of Truth is exactness, reality, undeviating certitude. Why, then, the ceaseless conflict between the religions and creeds? Is it not because of error? Contradiction and conflict belong to the domain of error, for error, being confusion, is in the nature of self-contradiction. If the Christian says, "My religion is true and Buddhism is false," and if the Buddhist says, "Christianity is false and Buddhism is true," we are at once confronted with an irreconcilable contradiction, for these two religions cannot be both true and false. Such a contradiction cannot spring from Truth, and must therefore spring from error. But if both these religious partisans should now say, or think, "Yes, truly the contradiction springs from error, but the error is in the other man and his religion, and not in me and mine," this does but intensify the contradiction. Whence, then, springs the error, and where is Truth? Does not the very attitude of mind which these men adopt toward each other constitute the error? and were they to reverse that attitude, exchanging antagonism for good-will, would they not perceive the Truth which does not stand in conflict with itself?

The man who says, "My religion is true, and my neighbor's is false," has not yet discovered the truth in his own religion, for when a man has done that, he will see Truth in all religions. As behind all the universal phenomena there is but one Truth, so behind all the religions and creeds there is but one religion, for every religion contains the same ethical teaching, and all the Great Teachers taught exactly the same thing.

The precepts of the Sermon on the Mount are to be found in all religions, and the life which those precepts demand was lived by all the Great Teachers and many of their disciples, for the Truth is a pure heart and a blameless life, and not a set of dogmas and opinions. All religions teach purity of heart, holiness of life, compassion, love, and good-will; they teach the doing of good deeds and the giving up of selfishness and sin. These things are not dogmas, theologies, and opinions, they are things to be done, to be practised, to be lived. Men do not differ about these things, for they are the acknowledged verities in every sect. What, then, do they differ about? About their opinions, their speculations, their theologies.

Men differ about that which is unreal, not that which is real; they fight over error, and not over Truth. The very essential of all religion (and religions) is that before a man can know anything of Truth, he must cease from fighting his fellow-man, and shall learn to regard him with good-will and love; and how can a man do this while he is convinced that his neighbor's religion is false, and that it is his duty to do all that he can to undermine and overthrow it? This is not doing unto others as we would that they should do to us.

That which is true and real is true and real everywhere and always. There is no distinction between the pious Christian and the pious Buddhist. Purity of heart, piety of life, holy aspirations, and the love of Truth are the same in the Buddhist as the Christian. The good deeds of the Buddhist are not different from the good deeds of the Christian. Remorse for sin and sorrow for wrong thoughts and deeds spring in the hearts, not only of Christians, but men of all religions. Great is the need of sympathy. Great is the need of love.

All religions are the same in that they teach the same fundamental verities, but men, instead of practising these verities, engage in opinions and speculations about things which are outside the range of knowledge and experience, and it is in defending and promulgating their own particular speculations that men become divided and engage in conflict with each other.

Condemnation is incipient persecution. The thought, "I am right and you are wrong," is a seed prolific of hatred. It was out of this seed that the Spanish Inquisition grew. He who would find the universal Truth must abandon egotism, must quench the hateful flames of condemnation, and, taking out of his heart the baneful thought, "All others are wrong," must think the illuminating thought, "It is I who am wrong," and having thus thought, he will cease from sin, and will live in love and good-will toward all, making no distinctions, engaging in no divisions, a peacemaker and not a partisan. Thus living charitably disposed toward all, he will become one with all, and will comprehend the Universal Truth, the Eternal Religion; for while error refutes error and selfishness divides, Truth demonstrates Truth and Religion unifies.

Light on Law and Miracle

The love of the wonderful is an element in human nature, which, like passions and desires, requires to be curbed, directed, and finally transmuted; otherwise superstition and the obscuration of reason and insight cannot be avoided. The idea of miracle must be transcended before the orderly, eternal, and beneficent nature of law can be perceived, and that peace and certainty which a knowledge of law bestows can be enjoyed.

Just as a child when its eyes are opened to the phenomena of this world becomes involved in wonder, and revels in tales of giants and fairies, so when a man first opens his mental eyes to spiritual things does he become involved in stories of marvels and miracles; and as the child at last becomes a man and leaves behind him the crudities of childhood, understanding more accurately the relative nature of the phenomena around him, so with a fuller spiritual development and greater familiarity with the inner realities, a man at last leaves behind him the era of childish wonderment, comes into touch with the laws of things, and governs his life by principles that are fixed and invariable.

Law is universal and eternal, and, although vast areas of knowledge are waiting to be revealed, cause and effect will ever prevail, and every new discovery, every truth revealed, will serve to bring men nearer to a realization of the beauty, stability, and supremacy of law. And very gladdening it is to know that law is inviolable and eternal throughout every department of nature, for then we know that the operations of the universe are ever the same, and can therefore be discovered, understood, and obeyed. This is a ground of certainty, and therefore of great hope and joy. The idea of miracle is a denial of law and the substitution of an arbitrary and capricious power.

It is true that around the lives of the Great Teachers of humanity stories of miracle have grown, but they have emanated from the undeveloped minds of the people, and not from the Teachers themselves. Lao-Tze expounded the Supreme Law, or Reason, which admits of no miracle, yet his religion has, today, become so corrupted with the introduction of the marvellous as to be little better than a mass of superstition. Even Buddhism, whose founder declared that, "Seeing that the Law of Karma (cause and effect) governs all things, the disciple who aims at performing miracles does not understand the doctrine," and that "The desire to perform miracles arises either from covetousness or vanity," has surrounded, in its corrupted form, the life of its Great Master with a number of miracles. Even during the lifetime of Ramakrishna, the Hindu teacher who died in 1886, and who is regarded by his disciples as an incarnation of Deity to this age, all sorts of miracles were attributed to him by the people, and are now associated with his name; yet, according to Max Müller, these miracles are without any foundation of evidence or fact, and Ramakrishna himself ridiculed and repudiated miracle.

As men become more enlightened, miracles and wonder-working will be expunged from religion, and the orderly beauty of Law and the ethical grandeur of obedience to Law will become revealed and known. No man who desires to perform miracles or astral or psychological wonders, who is curious to see invisible or supernatural beings, or who is ambitious to become a "Master" or an "Adept," can attain a clear perception of Truth and the living of the highest life. Childish wonderment about things must be supplanted by knowledge of things, and vanity is a complete barrier to the entrance of the true path which demands of the disciple lowliness of heart, humility. He is on the true path who is cultivating kindliness, forbearance, and a loving heart; and the marks of the true Master are not miracles and wonder-working, but Infinite patience, boundless compassion, spotless purity, and a heart at peace with all.

Light on War and Peace

War springs from inward strife. "War in heaven" precedes war on earth. When the inward spiritual harmony is destroyed by division and conflict, it will manifest itself outwardly in the form of war. Without this inward conflict war could not be, nor can war cease until the inward harmony is restored.

War consists of aggression and resistance, and after the fight has commenced both combatants are alike aggressors and resisters. Thus the effort to put an end to war by aggressive means produces war. "I have set myself stubbornly against the war spirit," said a man a short time ago. He did not know that he was, by that attitude of mind, practising and fostering the war spirit.

To fight against war is to produce war. It is impossible to fight for peace, because all fighting is the annihilation of peace. To think of putting an end to war by denouncing and fighting it is the same as if one should try to quench fire by throwing straw upon it. He, therefore, who is truly a man of peace, does not resist war, but practises peace. He who takes sides and practises attack and defence, is responsible for war, for he is always at war in his mind. He cannot know the nature of peace, for he has not arrived at peace in his own heart. The true man of peace is he who has put away from his mind the spirit of quarreling and party strife, who neither attacks others nor defends himself, and whose heart is at peace with all. Such a man has already laid in his heart the foundations of the empire of peace; he is a peace maker, for he is at peace with the whole world and practises the spirit of peace under all circumstances.

Very beautiful is the spirit of peace, and it says, "Come and rest." Bickerings, quarrellings, party divisions—these must be forever abandoned by him who would establish peace.

War will continue so long as men will allow themselves, individually, to be dominated by passion, and only when men have quelled the inward tumult will the outward horror pass away.

Self is the great enemy, the producer of all strife, and the maker of many sorrows; he, therefore, who will bring about peace on earth, let him overcome egotism, let him subdue his passions, let him conquer himself.

Light on the Brotherhood of Man

There is no lack of writing and preaching about "universal brotherhood," and it has been adopted as a leading article of faith by many newly formed societies; but what is so urgently needed to begin with, is not universal brotherhood, but *particular Brotherhood*, that is, the adoption of a magnanimous, charitable, and kindly spirit toward those with whom we come in immediate contact; toward those who contradict, oppose and attack us, as well as toward those who love and agree with us.

I make a very simple statement of truth when I say that until such particular brotherhood is practised, universal brotherhood will remain a meaningless term, for universal brotherhood is an end, a goal, and the way to it is by particular brotherhood; the one is a sublime and far-reaching consummation, the other is the means by which that consummation must be realized.

I remember on one occasion reading a paper devoted largely to the teaching of universal brotherhood, and the leading article—a long and learned one—was an exposition of this subject; but on turning over a few more pages, I found another piece by the same writer in which he accused of misrepresentation, lying, and selfishness, not his enemies, but the brethren of his own Society, who bear, at least as far as such sins are concerned, stainless reputations.

A scriptural writer has asked the question, "If a man love not his brother whom he hath seen, how can he love God whom he hath not seen?" In the same manner, if a man does not love the brother whom he knows, how can he love men of all creeds and all nations whom he does not know?

To write articles on universal brotherhood is one thing; to live in peace with one's relations and neighbors and to return good for evil is quite another.

To endeavor to propagate universal brotherhood while fostering in our heart some sparks of envy, spite, resentment, malice, or hatred, is to be self-deluded; for thus shall we be all the time hindering and denying, by our actions, that which we eulogize by our words; but so subtle is such self-delusion, that, until the very heights of love and wisdom are reached, we are all liable at any moment to fall into it.

It is not because our fellow-men do not hold our views, or follow our religion, or see as we see, that universal brotherhood remains unrealized, but because of the prevalence of ill-will; and if we hate, avoid, and condemn others because they differ from us, or treat selfishly and harshly those who are near to us, all that we may say or do in the cause of universal brotherhood will be only another snare to our feet, a mockery to our aspirations, and a farce to the world at large.

Let us, then, remove all hatred and malice from our hearts; let us be filled with good-will toward those who try and test us by their immediate nearness; let us love them that hate us, and think magnanimously of those who condemn us or our doctrine—in a word, let us take the first step toward universal brotherhood, by practising brotherhood in the place where we now are, and toward those with whom we associate, which is the place where it is most needed; and as we succeed in being brotherly in these important particulars, universal brotherhood will be found to be not far distant.

Light on
Life's Sorrows

There is great sorrow in the world. This is one of the supreme facts of life. Grief and affliction visit every heart, and many that are today revelling in hilarious joy or sinful riot, will tomorrow be smitten low with sorrow. Suddenly, and with swift and silent certainty, comes its poignant arrow, entering the human heart, slaying its joy, laying low its hopes, and shattering all its earthly plans and prospects. Then the humbled, smitten soul reflects, and enters deeply and sympathetically into the hidden meanings of human life.

In the dark times of sorrow, men approach very near to Truth. When in one brief hour the builded hopes of many years of toil fall like a toy palace, and all earthly pleasures burst and vanish like petty bubbles in the grasp, then the crushed spirit, bewildered, tempest-tossed, and without a refuge, gropes in dumb anguish for the Eternal, and seeks its abiding peace.

"Blessed are they that mourn," said the Teacher of the West, and the Teacher of the East declared that "Where there is great suffering there is great bliss." Both these sayings express the truth that sorrow is a teacher and a purifier. Sorrow is not the end of life—though it is, in its consummation, the end of the worldly life—but it is the beginning of the heavenly life; it leads the bewildered spirit into rest and safety; for the end of sorrow is joy and peace.

Strong searcher for Truth! Strenuous fighter against self and passion! seasons of sorrow must be your portion for a time. While any vestige of self remains, temptations will assail you, and the veil of illusion will cloud your spiritual vision, producing sorrow and unrest; and when heavy clouds settle down upon your spirit, accept the darkness as your own, and pass through it bravely into the cloudless light beyond.

Bear well in mind that nothing can overtake you that does not belong to you and that is not for your eternal good. As the poet has truly sung—

*Nor space nor time, nor deep nor high Can keep
    my own away from me.*

And not alone are the bright things of life yours; the dark things are yours also. When difficulties and troubles gather thickly about you; when failures come and friends fall away; when the tongue that sweetly praised you, bitterly blames; when beloved lips that pressed upon your lips the soft, warm kisses of love, taunt and mock you in the lonely hour of your solitary grief; or when you lay beneath the sod the cold casket of clay that but yesterday held the responsive spirit of your beloved,—when these things overtake you, remember that the hour of your Gethsemane has come, that the cup of anguish is yours to drink. Drink it silently and murmur not, for in that hour of oppressive darkness and blinding pain no prayer will save you, no cry to heaven will bring you sweet relief; but faith and patience only will give you the strength to endure, and to go through your crucifixion with a meek and gentle spirit, not complaining, blaming no one, but accepting it as your own.

When one has reached the lowest point of sorrow; when, weak and exhausted, and overcome with a sense of powerlessness, he cries to God for help, and there comes no answering comfort and no succor—then, discovering the painfulness of sorrow and the insufficiency of prayer alone, he is ready to enter the path of self-renunciation, ready to purify his heart, ready to practice self-control, ready to become a spiritual athlete, and to develop that divine and invincible strength which is born of self-mastery.

He will find the cause of sorrow in his own heart, and will remove it. He will learn to stand alone; not craving sympathy from any, but giving it to all. Not thoughtlessly sinning and remorsefully repenting, but studying how not to commit sin. Humbled by innumerable defeats, and chastened by many sufferings, he will learn how to act blamelessly toward others, how to be gently and strong, kind and steadfast, compassionate and wise.

Thus he will gradually rise above sorrow, and at last Truth will dawn upon his mind, and he will understand the meaning of abiding peace. His mental eye will open to perceive the Cosmic Order. He will be blessed with the Vision of the Law, and will receive the Beatific Bliss.

When the true order of things is perceived, sorrow is transcended. When the contracted personal self which hugs its own little fleeting pleasures and broods over its own petty disappointments and dissatisfactions is broken up and cast away, then the larger life of Truth enters the mind, bringing bliss and peace; and the Universal Will takes the place of self. The individual becomes one with humanity. He forgets self in his love for all. His sorrow is swallowed up in the bliss of Truth.

Thus when you have, by experience, entered completely into the sorrow that is never lifted from the heart of mankind; when you have reaped and eaten all the bitter fruits of your own wrong thoughts and deeds—then divine compassion for all suffering beings will be born in your heart, healing all your wounds and drying all your tears. You will rise again into a new and heavenly life, where the sting of sorrow cannot enter, for there is no self there. After the crucifixion comes the transfiguration; the sorrowless state is reached through sorrow, and "the wise do not grieve."

Ever remember this—in the midst of sin and sorrow there abides the world of Truth. Redemption is at hand. The troubled may find peace; the impure may find purity. Healing awaits the broken-hearted; the weak will be adorned with strength, and the downtrodden will be lifted up and glorified.

Light on Life's Changes

The tendency of things to advance from a lower to a higher level, and from high to higher still, is universal. The worlds exist in order that beings may experience, and by experiencing, acquire knowledge and increase in wisdom.

Evolution is only another word for progress. It signifies perpetual change, but a purposeful change, a change accompanied by growth. Evolution does not mean the creation of a new being from a being of a different order; it means the modification of beings by experience and change; and such modification is progress.

The fact of change is ever before us. Nothing can escape it. Plants, animals, and men germinate, reach maturity, and pass into decay. Even the lordly suns and their attendant worlds rolling through illimitable spaces, although their life is reckoned in millions of years, at last decay and perish after having passed through innumerable changes. We cannot say of any being or object—"This will remain forever as it is," for even while we are saying it, the being or object would be undergoing change.

Sadness and suffering accompany this change; and beings mourn for that which has departed, for the things which are lost and gone. Yet in reality change is good, for it is the open door to all achievement, advancement and perfection.

Mind, as well as matter, is subject to the same change. Every experience, every thought, every deed, changes a man. There is little resemblance between the old man and his period of childhood and youth.

An eternally fixed, unchangeable being is not known. Such a being may be assumed, but it is a postulate only. It is not within the range of human observation and knowledge. A being not subject to change would be a being outside progress.

There is a teaching which declares that man has a spiritual soul that is eternally pure, eternally unchanged, eternally perfect, and that the sinning, suffering, changing man as we see him is an illusion—that, indeed, the spiritual soul is *the* man, and the other is an unreality.

There is another teaching that affirms that man is eternally imperfect, that stainless purity can never be reached, and that perfection is an impossibility, an illusion.

It will be found that these two extremes have no relation to *human experience*. They are both of the nature of speculative metaphysics which stand in opposition to the *facts of life*; so much so that the adherents of these two extremes deny the existence of the commonest every-day facts of human experience. That which is assumed is regarded as real; the facts of life are declared to be unreal.

It is well to avoid both these extremes, and find the middle way of human experience. It is well to avoid opinions and speculations of our own or others, it is well to *refer to the facts of life*. We see that man passes through birth and growth and old age, that he experiences sin, sickness, and death; that he sorrows and suffers, aspires and rejoices; and that he is ever looking forward to greater purity and striving toward perfection. These are not opinions, speculations, or metaphysics—they are universal facts.

If man were already perfect, there were no need for him to be perfected, and all moral teaching would be useless and ridiculous. Moreover, a perfect being could not be subject to illusion and unreality.

On the other hand, if a man could never attain to purity and perfection, his aspirations and strivings would be useless. They would indeed be mockeries; and the heavenly perfection of saintly and divine men would have to be belittled and denied.

We see around us sin and sorrow and suffering; and we see before us, in the lives of the great teachers, the sinless, sorrowless, divine state. Therefore, we know that man is an imperfect being, yet capable of, and destined for, perfection. The divine state toward which he aspires, he will reach. The fact that he so ardently desires it, means that he can reach it, even if the fact were not demonstrated in those great ones who have already attained.

Man is not a compound of two beings, one real and perfect, the other unreal and imperfect. He is one and real, and his experiences are real. His imperfection is apparent, and his advancement and progress are also apparent.

The realities of life claim men in spite of their metaphysics, and all come under the same law of change and progress. He who affirms the eternal sinlessness and perfection of man, should not, to be logical and consistent, ever speak of sins and faults, of disease and death; yet he refers to these things as matters to be dealt with. Thus in theory he denies the existence of that which he habitually recognizes in practice.

He also who denies the possibility of perfection, should not aspire or strive; yet we find him practising self-denial and striving ceaselessly toward perfection.

Holding to the theoretical does not absolve men from the inevitable. The teacher of the unreality of sickness, old age, and death is at last caught in the toils of disease, succumbs to age, and disappears in death.

Change is not only inevitable, it is constant and unvarying law. Without it, everything would remain forever as it is, and there could be neither growth nor progress.

The strenuous struggle of all life is a prophecy of its perfection. The lookings upward of all beings is evidence of their ceaseless ascension. Aspirations, ideals, moral aims, while they denote man's imperfection, assuredly point to his future perfection. They are neither unnecessary nor aimless, but are woven into the fabric of things; they belong to the vital essence of the universe.

Whatsoever a man believes or disbelieves, what theories he holds or does not hold, one thing is certain—he is found in the stream of life, and *must* think and act; and to think and act is to experience; and to experience is to change and develop.

That man is conscious of sin, means that he can become pure; that he abhors evil, signifies that he can reach up to Good; that he is a pilgrim in the land of error, assures us, without doubt, that he will at last come to the beautiful city of Truth.

Light on
the Truth of
Transitoriness

It is well sometimes to meditate deeply and seriously on the truth of Transitoriness. By meditation we will come to perceive how all compounded things must pass away; yea, how even while they remain they are already in process of passing away. Such meditation will soften the heart, deepen the understanding, and render one more fully conscious of the sacred nature of life.

What is there that does not pass away, among all the things of which a man says, "This will be mine to-morrow"? Even the mind is continually changing. Old characteristics die and pass away, and new ones are formed. In the midst of life all things are dying. Nothing endures; nothing can be retained. Things appear and then disappear; they become, and then they pass away.

The ancient sages declared the visible universe to be Mâyâ, illusion, meaning thereby that impermanency is the antithesis of Reality. Change and decay are in the very nature of visible things, and they are unreal—illusory—in the sense that they pass away forever.

He who would ascend into the realm of Reality, who would penetrate into the world of Truth, must first perceive, with no uncertain vision, the transitory nature of the things of life; he must cease to delude himself into believing that he can retain his hold on his possessions, his body, his pleasures and objects of pleasure; for as the flower fades and as the leaves of the tree fall and wither, so must these things, in their season, pass away for ever.

The perception of the Truth of Transitoriness is one of the first great steps in wisdom, for when it is fully grasped, and its lesson has sunk deeply into the heart, the clinging to perishable things which is the cause of all sorrow, will be yielded up, and the search for the Truth which abides will be accelerated.

Anguish is rife because men set their hearts on the acquisition of things that perish, because they lust for the possession of those things which even when obtained cannot be retained.

There is no sorrow that would not vanish if the clinging to evanescent things were given up; there is no grief that would not be dispersed if the desire to have and to hold those things which in their very nature cannot endure, were taken out of the heart.

Tens of thousands of grief-stricken hearts are today bewailing the loss of some loved object which they called theirs in days that are past, are weeping over that which is gone forever and cannot be restored.

Men are slow to learn the lessons of experience and to acquire wisdom, and unnumbered griefs and pains and sorrows have failed to impress them with the Truth of Transitoriness. He who clings to that which is impermanent, cannot escape sorrow, and the intensity of his sorrow will be measured by the strength of his clinging. He who sets his heart on perishable things embraces the companionship of grief and lamentation.

Men cannot find wisdom because they will not renounce the clinging to things, because they believe that the clinging to perishable objects is the source of happiness, and not the cause of sorrow; they cannot escape unrest and enter into the life of peace because desire is difficult to quench, and the immediate and transitory pleasure which gratified desire affords is mistaken for abiding joy.

It is because the true order of things is not understood that grief is universal; it is ignorance of the fleeting nature of things that lies at the root of sorrow.

The sting of anguish will be taken out of life when the lust to hold and to preserve the things of decay is taken out of the heart.

Sorrow is ended for him who sees things as they are; who, realizing the nature of transiency, detaches his heart and mind from the things that perish.

There is a right use for perishable things, and when they are rightly used, and not doted upon for themselves alone, their loss will cause no sorrow.

If a rich man thinks in his heart, "My riches and possessions are no part of me, nor can I call them mine, seeing that when I am summoned to depart from this world, I cannot take them with me; they are entrusted to me to use rightly, and I will employ them to the best of my ability for the good of men and for the world," such a man, though surrounded by luxuries and responsibilities, will be lifted above sorrow, and will draw near to Truth. On the other hand, if the poor man does not covet riches and possessions, his condition will cause him no anxiety and unrest.

He who by a right understanding of life rids his heart of all selfish grasping and clinging, who uses everything wisely and in its proper place, and who, with chastened heart, and mind clarified of all thirsty desires, remains serene and self-contained in the midst of all changes, such a man will find Truth, he will stand face to face with Reality.

For in the midst of all error there abides the Truth; at the heart of transiency there reposes the Permanent; and illusion does but veil the eternal and unchanging Reality.

The nature of that Reality it is not my purpose to deal with here; let it suffice that I indicate that it is only found by abandoning, in the heart, all that is not of Love and Compassion and Wisdom and Purity. In these things there is no element of transitoriness, no sorrow, and no unrest.

When the truth of Transitoriness is well perceived, and when the lesson contained in the truth of Transitoriness is well learned, then does a man set out to find the abiding Truth; then does he wean his heart from those selfish elements which are productive of sorrow.

He whose treasure is Truth, who fashions his life in accordance with Wisdom, will find the Joy which does not pass away, will leave behind him the land of lamentation, and, crossing the wide ocean of illusion, will come to the Sorrowless Shore.

The Light That Never Goes Out

Amid the multitude of conflicting opinions and theories, and caught in the struggle of existence, whither shall the confused truthseeker turn to find the path that leads to peace unending? To what refuge shall he fly from the uncertainties and sorrows of change?

Will he find peace in pleasure? Pleasure has its place, and in its place it is good; but as an end, as a refuge, it affords no shelter, and he who seeks it as such does but increase the anguish of life; for what is more fleeting than pleasure, and what is more empty than the heart that seeks satisfaction in so ephemeral a thing? There is, therefore, no abiding refuge in pleasure.

Will he find peace in wealth and worldly success? Wealth and worldly success have their place, but they are fickle and uncertain possessions, and he who seeks them for themselves alone will be burdened with many anxieties and cares; and when the storms of adversity sweep over his glittering yet frail habitation, he will find himself helpless and exposed. But even should he maintain such possessions throughout life, what satisfaction will they afford him in the hour of death? There is no abiding refuge in wealth and worldly success.

Will he find peace in health? Health has its place, and it should not be thrown away or despised, but it belongs to the body which is destined for dissolution, and is therefore perishable. Even should health be maintained for a hundred years, the time will come when the physical energies will decline and debility and decay will overtake them. There is no abiding refuge in health.

Will he find refuge in those whom he dearly loves? Those whom he loves have their place in his life. They afford him means of practising unselfishness, and therefore of arriving at Truth. He should cherish them with loving care, and consider their needs before his own; but the time will come when they will be separated from him, and he will be left alone. There is no abiding refuge in loved ones.

Will he find peace in this Scripture or that? Scripture fills an important place. As a guide it is good, but it cannot be a refuge, for one may know the Scripture by heart, and yet be in sore conflict and unrest. The theories of men are subject to successive changes, and no limit can be set to the variety of textual interpretations. There is no abiding refuge in Scripture.

Will he find rest in this teacher or that? The teacher has his place, and as an instructor he renders good service. But teachers are numerous, and their differences are many; though one may regard his particular teacher as in possession of Truth, that teacher will one day be taken from him. There is no abiding refuge in a teacher.

Will he find peace in solitude? Solitude is good and necessary in its place, but he who courts it as a lasting refuge will be like one perishing of thirst in a waterless desert. He will escape men and the turmoil of the city, but he will not escape himself and the unrest of his heart. There is no abiding rest in solitude.

If, then, the seeker can find no refuge in pleasure, in success, in health, in friends, in Scripture, in the teacher, or in solitude, whither shall he turn to find that sanctuary which shall afford abiding peace?

Let him take refuge in righteousness; let him fly to the sanctuary of a purified heart. Let him enter the pathway of a blameless, stainless life, and walk it meekly and patiently until it brings him to the eternal temple of Truth in his own heart.

He who has taken refuge in Truth, even in the habitation of a wise understanding and a loving and steadfast heart, is the same whether in pleasure or pain; wealth or poverty; success or failure; health or sickness; with friends or without; in solitude or noisy haunts; and he is independent of bibles and teachers, for the Spirit of Truth instructs him. He perceives, without fear or sorrow, the change and decay which are in all things. He has found peace; he has entered the abiding sanctuary; he knows the Light that will never go out.

Man: King
of Mind,
Body, *and*
Circumstance

Within, around, above, below,
    The primal forces burn and brood,
Awaiting wisdom's guidance; lo!
    All their material is good:
Evil subsists in their abuse;
Good, in their wise and lawful use.

Contents

Foreword

The problem of life consists in learning how to live. It is like the problem of addition or subtraction to the schoolboy. When mastered, all difficulty disappears, and the problem has vanished. All the problems of life, whether they be social, political, or religious, subsist in ignorance and wrong-living. As they are solved in the heart of each individual, they will be solved in the mass of men. Humanity at present is in the painful stage of "learning." It is confronted with the difficulties of its own ignorance. As men learn to live rightly, learn to direct their forces and use their functions and faculties by the light of wisdom, the sum of life will be correctly done, and its mastery will put an end to all the "problems of evil." To the wise, all such problems have ceased.

—James Allen
Bryngoleu,
Ilfracombe, England

The Inner World
of Thoughts

Man is the maker of happiness and misery. Further, he is the creator and perpetuator of his own happiness and misery. These things are not externally imposed; they are internal conditions. Their cause is neither deity, nor devil, nor circumstance, but Thought. They are the effects of deeds, and deeds are the visible side of thoughts. Fixed attitudes of mind determine courses of conduct, and from courses of conduct come those reactions called *happiness* and *unhappiness*. This being so, it follows that, to alter the reactive condition, one must alter the active thought. To exchange misery for happiness, it is necessary to reverse the fixed attitude of mind and habitual course of conduct which is the cause of misery, and the reverse effect will appear in the mind and life. A man has no power to be happy while thinking and acting selfishly; he cannot be unhappy while thinking and acting unselfishly. Wheresoever the cause is, there the effect will appear. Man cannot abrogate effects, but he can alter causes. He can purify his nature; he can remould his character. There is great power in self-conquest; there is great joy in transforming oneself.

Each man is circumscribed by his own thoughts, but he can gradually extend their circle; he can enlarge and elevate his mental sphere. He can leave the low, and reach up to the high; he can refrain from harbouring thoughts that are dark and hateful, and can cherish thoughts that are bright and beautiful; and as he does this, he will pass into a higher sphere of power and beauty, will become conscious of a more complete and perfect world.

For men live in spheres low or high according to the nature of their thoughts. Their world is as dark and narrow as they conceive it to be, as expansive and glorious as their comprehensive capacity. Everything around them is tinged with the colour of their thoughts.

Consider the man whose mind is suspicious, covetous, envious. How small and mean and drear everything appears to him. Having no grandeur in himself, he sees no grandeur anywhere; being ignoble himself, he is incapable of seeing nobility in any being. Even his god is a covetous being that can be bribed, and he judges all men and women to be just as petty and selfish as he himself is, so that he sees in the most exalted acts of unselfishness only motives that are mean and base.

Consider again the man whose mind is unsuspecting, generous, magnanimous. How wondrous and beautiful is his world. He is conscious of some kind of nobility in all creatures and beings. He sees men as true, and to him they are true. In his presence the meanest forget their nature, and for the moment become like himself, getting a glimpse, albeit confused, in that temporary upliftment, of a higher order of things, of an immeasurably nobler and happier life.

That small-minded man and this large-hearted man live in two different worlds, though they be neighbours. Their consciousness embraces totally different principles. Their actions are each the reverse of the other. Their moral insight is contrary. They each look out upon a different order of things. Their mental spheres are separate, and, like two detached circles, they never mingle. The one is in hell, the other in heaven, as truly as they will ever be, and death will not place a greater gulf between them than already exists. To the one, the world is a den of thieves; to the other, it is the dwelling-place of gods. The one keeps a revolver handy, and is always on his guard against being robbed or cheated (unconscious of the fact that he is all the time robbing and cheating himself), the other keeps ready a banquet for the best. He throws open his doors to talent, beauty, genius, goodness. His friends are of the aristocracy of character. They have become a part of himself. They are in his sphere of thought, his world of consciousness. From his heart pours forth nobility, and it returns to him tenfold in the multitude of those who love him and do him honour.

The natural grades in human society—what are they but spheres of thought, and modes of conduct manifesting those spheres? The proletariat may rail against these divisions, but he will not alter or affect them. There is no artificial remedy for equalizing states of thought having no natural affinity, and separated by the fundamental principles of life. The lawless and the law-abiding are eternally apart, nor is it hatred nor pride that separates them, but states of intelligence and modes of conduct which in the moral principles of things stand mutually unrelated. The rude and ill-mannered are shut out from the circle of the gentle and refined by the impassable wall of their own mentality which, though they may remove by patient self-improvement, they can never scale by a vulgar intrusion. The kingdom of heaven is not taken by violence, but he who conforms to its principles receives the password. The ruffian moves in a society of ruffians; the saint is one of an elect brethren whose communion is divine music. All men are mirrors reflecting according to their own surface. All men, looking at the world of men and things, are looking into a mirror which gives back their own reflection.

Each man moves in the limited or expansive circle of his own thoughts, and all outside that circle is non-existent to him. He only knows that which he has become. The narrower the boundary, the more convinced is the man that there is no further limit, no other circle. The lesser cannot contain the greater, and he has no means of apprehending the larger minds; such knowledge comes only by growth. The man who moves in a widely extended circle of thought knows all the lesser circles from which he has emerged, for in the larger experience all lesser experiences are contained and preserved; and when his circle impinges upon the sphere of perfect manhood, when he is fitting himself for company and communion with them of blameless conduct and profound understanding, then his wisdom will have become sufficient to convince him that there are wider circles still beyond of which he is as yet but dimly conscious, or is entirely ignorant.

Men, like schoolboys, find themselves in standards or classes to which their ignorance or knowledge entitles them. The curriculum of the sixth standard is a mystery to the boy in the first; it is outside and beyond the circle of his comprehension; but he reaches it by persistent effort and patient growth in learning. By mastering and outgrowing all the standards between, he comes at last to the sixth, and makes its learning his own; and beyond still is the sphere of the teacher. So in life, men whose deeds are dark and selfish, full of passion and personal desire, cannot comprehend those whose deeds are bright and unselfish, whose minds are calm, deep, and pure, but they can reach this higher standard, this enlarged consciousness, by effort in right-doing, by growth in thought and moral comprehension. And above and beyond all lower and higher standards stand the Teachers of mankind, the Cosmic Masters, the Saviours of the world whom the adherents of the various religions worship. There are grades in teachers as in pupils, and some there are who have not yet reached the rank and position of *Master*, yet, by the sterling morality of their character, are guides and teachers; but to occupy a pulpit or rostrum does not make a man a teacher. A man is constituted a teacher by virtue of that moral greatness which calls forth the respect and reverence of mankind.

Each man is as low or high, as little or great, as base or noble, as his thoughts; no more, no less. Each moves within the sphere of his own thoughts, and that sphere is his world. In that world in which he forms his habits of thought, he finds his company. He dwells in the region which harmonizes with his particular growth. But he need not perforce remain in the lower worlds. He can lift his thoughts and ascend. He can pass above and beyond into higher realms, into happier habitations. When he chooses and wills he can break the carapace of selfish thought, and breathe the purer airs of a more expansive life.

The Outer World
of Things

The world of things is the other half of the world of thoughts. The inner informs the outer. The greater embraces the lesser. Matter is the counterpart of mind. Events are streams of thought. Circumstances are combinations of thought, and the outer conditions and actions of others in which each man is involved are intimately related to his own mental needs and development. Man is a part of his surroundings. He is not separate from his fellows, but is bound closely to them by the peculiar intimacy and interaction of deeds, and by those fundamental laws of thought which are the roots of human society.

One cannot alter external things to suit his passing whims and wishes, but he can set aside his whims and wishes; he can so alter his attitude of mind toward externals that they will assume a different aspect. He cannot mould the actions of others toward him, but he can rightly fashion his actions toward them. He cannot break down the wall of circumstance by which he is surrounded, but he can wisely adapt himself to it, or find the way out into enlarged circumstances by extending his mental horizon. Things follow thoughts. Alter your thoughts, and things will receive a new adjustment. To reflect truly, the mirror must be true. A warped glass gives back an exaggerated image. A disturbed mind gives a distorted reflection of the world. Subdue the mind, organize and tranquilize it, and a more beautiful image of the universe, a more perfect perception of the world-order, will be the result.

Man has all power within the world of his own mind, to purify and perfect it, but his power in the outer world of other minds is subject and limited. This is made plain when we reflect that each finds himself in a world of men and things, a unit amongst myriads of similar units. These units do not act independently and despotically, but responsively and sympathetically. My fellow-men are involved in my actions, and they will deal with them. If what I do be a menace to them, they will adopt protective measures against me. As the human body expels its morbid atoms, so the body politic instinctively expurgates its recalcitrant members. Your wrong acts are so many wounds inflicted on this body politic, and the healing of its wounds will be your pain and sorrow. This ethical cause and effect is not different from that physical cause and effect with which the simplest is acquainted. It is but an extension of the same law; its application to the larger body of humanity. No act is aloof. Your most secret deed is invisibly reported, its good being protected in joy, its evil destroyed in pain. There is a great ethical truth in the old fable of "the Book of Life," in which every thought and deed is recorded and judged. It is because of this—that your deed belongs, not alone to yourself, but to humanity and the universe— that you are powerless to avert external effects, but are all-powerful to modify and correct internal causes; and it is also because of this that the perfecting of one's own deeds is man's highest duty and most sublime accomplishment.

The obverse of this truth—that you are powerless to obviate external things and deeds—is, that external things and deeds are powerless to injure you. The cause of your bondage as of your deliverance is within. The injury that comes to you through others is the rebound of your own deed, the reflex of your own mental attitude. *They* are the instruments, you are the cause. Destiny is ripened deeds. The fruit of life, both bitter and sweet, is received by each man in just measure. The righteous man is free. None can injure him; none can destroy him; none can rob him of his peace. His attitude toward men, born of understanding, disarms their power to wound him. Any injury which they may try to inflict, rebounds upon themselves to their own hurt, leaving him unharmed and untouched. The good that goes from him is his perennial fount of happiness, his eternal source of strength. Its root is serenity, its flower is joy.

The harm which a man sees in the action of another toward him—say, for instance, an act of slander—is not in the act itself, but in his attitude of mind toward it; the injury and unhappiness are created by himself, and subsist in his lack of understanding concerning the nature and power of deeds. He thinks the act can permanently injure or ruin his character, whereas it is utterly void of any such power; the reality being that the deed can only injure or ruin the doer of it. Thinking himself injured, the man becomes agitated and unhappy, and takes great pains to counteract the supposed harm to himself, and these very pains give the slander an appearance of truth, and aid rather than hinder it. All his agitation and unrest is created by his reception of the deed, and not actually by the deed itself. The righteous man has proved this by the fact that the same act has ceased to arouse in him any disturbance. He understands, and therefore ignores it. It belongs to a sphere which he has ceased to inhabit, to a region of consciousness with which he has no longer any affinity. He does not receive the act into himself, the thought of injury to himself being absent. He lives above the mental darkness in which such acts thrive, and they can no more injure or disturb him than a boy can injure or divert the sun by throwing stones at it. It was to emphasize this that Buddha, to the end of his days, never ceased to tell his disciples that so long as the thought "I have been injured," or "I have been cheated," or "I have been insulted," could arise in a man's mind, he had not comprehended the Truth.

And as with the conduct of others, so is it with external things—with surroundings and circumstances—in themselves they are neither good nor bad, it is the mental attitude and state of heart that makes them so. A man imagines he could do great things if he were not hampered by circumstances—by want of money, want of time, want of influence, and want of freedom from family ties. In reality the man is not hindered by these things at all. He, in his mind, ascribes to them a power which they do not possess, and he submits, not to them, but to his opinion about them, that is, to a weak element in his nature. The real "want" that hampers him is the *want of the right attitude of mind*. When he regards his circumstances as spurs to his resources, when he sees that his so-called "drawbacks" are the very steps up which he is to mount successfully to his achievement, then his necessity gives birth to invention, and the "hindrances" are transformed into *aids*. *The man* is the all-important factor. If his mind be wholesome and rightly tuned, he will not whine and whimper over his circumstances, but will rise up, and outgrow them. He who complains of his circumstances has not yet become a man, and Necessity will continue to prick and lash him till he rises into manhood's strength, and then she will submit to him. Circumstance is a severe taskmaster to the weak, an obedient servant to the strong.

It is not external things, but our thoughts about them, that bind us or set us free. We forge our own chains, build our own dungeons, take ourselves prisoners; or we loose our bonds, build our own palaces, or roam in freedom through all scenes and events. If I think that my surroundings are powerful to bind me, that thought will keep me bound. If I think that, in my thought and life, I can rise above my surroundings, that thought will liberate me. One should ask of his thoughts, "Are they leading to bondage or deliverance?" and he should abandon thoughts that bind, and adopt thoughts that set free.

If we fear our fellow-men, fear opinion, poverty, the withdrawal of friends and influence, then we are bound indeed, and cannot know the inward happiness of the enlightened, the freedom of the just; but if in our thoughts we are pure and free, if we see in life's reactions and reverses nothing to cause us trouble or fear, but everything to aid us in our progress, nothing remains that can prevent us from accomplishing the aims of our life, for then we are free indeed.

Habit: Its Slavery and Its Freedom

M an is subject to the law of habit. Is he then free? Yes, he is free. Man did not make life and its laws; they are eternal; he finds himself involved in them, and he can understand and obey them. Man's power does not enable him to make laws of being; it subsists in discrimination and choice. Man does not create one jot of the universal conditions or laws; they are the essential principles of things, and are neither made nor unmade. He discovers, not makes, them. Ignorance of them is at the root of the world's pain. To defy them is folly and bondage. Who is the freer man, the thief who defies the laws of his country, or the honest citizen who obeys them? Who, again, is the freer man, the fool who thinks he can live as he likes, or the wise man who chooses to do only that which is right?

Man is, in the nature of things, a being of habit, and this he cannot alter; but he can alter his habits. He cannot alter the law of his nature, but he can adapt his nature to the law. No man wishes to alter the law of gravitation, but all men adapt themselves to it; they use it by bending to it, not by defying or ignoring it. Men do not run up against walls or jump over precipices in the hope that this law will alter for them. They walk alongside walls, and keep clear of precipices.

Man can no more get outside the law of habit, than he can get outside the law of gravitation, but he can employ it wisely or unwisely. As scientists and inventors master the physical forces and laws by obeying and using them, so wise men master the spiritual forces and laws in the same way. While the bad man is the whipped slave of habit, the good man is its wise director and master. Not its maker, let me reiterate, nor yet its arbitrary commander, but its self-disciplined user, its master by virtue of knowledge grounded on obedience. He is the bad man whose habits of thought and action are bad. He is the good man whose habits of thought and action are good. The bad man becomes the good man by transforming or transmuting his habits. He does not alter the law; he alters himself; he adapts himself to the law. Instead of submitting to selfish indulgences, he obeys moral principles. He becomes the master of the lower by enlisting in the service of the higher. The law of habit remains the same, but he is changed from bad to good by his readjustment to the law.

Habit is *repetition*. Man repeats the same thoughts, the same actions, the same experiences over and over again until they are incorporated with his being, until they are built into his character as part of himself. Faculty is fixed habit. Evolution is mental accumulation. Man, today, is the result of millions of repetitious thoughts and acts. He is not ready-made, he becomes, and is still becoming. His character is predetermined by his own choice. The thought, the act, which he chooses, that, by habit, he becomes.

Thus each man is an accumulation of thoughts and deeds. The characteristics which he manifests instinctively and without effort are lines of thought and action become, by long repetition, automatic; for it is the nature of habit to become, at last, unconscious, to repeat, as it were, itself without any apparent choice or effort on the part of its possessor; and in due time it takes such complete possession of the individual as to appear to render his will powerless to counteract it. This is the case with all habits, whether good or bad; when bad, the man is spoken of as being the "victim" of a bad habit or a vicious mind; when good, he is referred to as having, by nature, a "good disposition."

All men are, and will continue to be, subject to their own habits, whether they be good or bad— that is, subject to their own reiterated and accumulated thoughts and deeds. Knowing this, the wise man chooses to subject himself to good habits, for such service is joy, bliss, and freedom; while to become subject to bad habits is misery, wretchedness, slavery.

This law of habit is beneficent, for while it enables a man to bind himself to the chains of slavish practices, it enables him to become so fixed in good courses as to do them unconsciously, to do instinctively that which is right, without restraint or exertion, and in perfect happiness and freedom. Observing this automatism in life, men have denied the existence of will or freedom on man's part. They speak of him as being "born" good or bad, and regard him as the helpless instrument of blind forces.

It is true that man is the instrument of mental forces—or to be more accurate, he is those forces—but they are not blind, and he can direct them, and redirect them into new channels. In a word, he can take himself in hand and reconstruct his habits; for though it is also true that he is born with a given character, that character is the product of numberless lives during which it has been slowly built up by choice and effort, and in this life it will be considerably modified by new experiences.

No matter how apparently helpless a man has become under the tyranny of a bad habit, or a bad characteristic—and they are essentially the same—he can, so long as sanity remains, break away from it and become free, replacing it by its opposite good habit; and when the good possesses him as the bad formerly did, there will be neither wish nor need to break from that, for its dominance will be perennial happiness, and not perpetual misery.

That which a man has formed within himself, he can break up and re-form when he so wishes and wills; and a man does not wish to abandon a bad habit so long as he regards it as pleasurable. It is when it assumes a painful tyranny over him that he begins to look for a way of escape, and finally abandons the bad for something better.

No man is helplessly bound. The very law by which he has become a self-bound slave will enable him to become a self-emancipated master. To know this, he has but to act upon it—that is, deliberately and strenuously to abandon the old lines of thought and conduct, and diligently fashion new and better lines. That he may not accomplish this in a day, a week, a month, a year, or five years, should not dishearten and dismay him. Time is required for the new repetitions to become established, and the old ones to be broken up; but the law of habit is certain and infallible, and a line of effort patiently pursued and never abandoned, is sure to be crowned with success; for if a bad condition, a mere negation, can become fixed and firm, how much more surely can a good condition, a positive principle, become established and powerful! A man is powerless to overcome the wrong and unhappy elements in himself only *so long as he regards himself as powerless.* If to the bad habit is added the thought, "I cannot," the bad habit will remain. Nothing can be overcome till the thought of powerlessness is uprooted and abolished from the mind. The great stumbling-block is not the habit itself, it is *the belief in the impossibility of overcoming it.* How can a man overcome a bad habit so long as he is convinced that it is impossible? How can a man be prevented from overcoming it when he knows that he can, and is determined to do it? The dominant thought by which man has enslaved himself is the thought, "I cannot overcome my sins." Bring this thought out into the light, in all its nakedness, and it is seen to be a belief in the power of evil, with its other pole, disbelief in the power of good. For a man to say, or believe, that he cannot rise above wrong-thinking and wrong-doing, is to submit to evil, is to abandon and renounce good.

By such thoughts, such beliefs, man binds himself; by their opposite thoughts, opposite beliefs, he sets himself free. A changed attitude of mind changes the character, the habits, the life. Man is his own deliverer. He has brought about his thraldom; he can bring about his emancipation. All through the ages he has looked, and is still looking, for an external deliverer, but he still remains bound. The Great Deliverer is within; He is the Spirit of Truth; and the Spirit of Truth is the Spirit of Good; and he is in the Spirit of Good who dwells habitually in good thoughts and their effects, good actions.

Man is not bound by any power outside his own wrong thoughts, and from these he can set himself free; and foremost, the enslaving thoughts from which he needs to be delivered are—"I cannot rise," "I cannot break away from bad habits," "I cannot alter my nature," "I cannot control and conquer myself," "I cannot cease from sin." All these "cannots" have no existence in the things to which they submit; they exist only in thought.

Such negations are bad thought-habits which need to be eradicated, and in their place should be planted the positive "I can," which should be tended and developed until it becomes a powerful tree of habit, bearing the good and life-giving fruit of right and happy living.

Habit binds us; habit sets us free. Habit is primarily in thought, secondarily in deed. Turn the thought from bad to good, and the deed will immediately follow. Persist in the bad, and it will bind you tighter and tighter; persist in the good, and it will take you into ever-widening spheres of freedom. He who loves his bondage, let him remain bound. He who thirsts for freedom, let him come and be set free.

Bodily Conditions

There are today scores of distinct schools devoted to the healing of the body; a fact which shows the great prevalence of physical suffering, as the hundreds of religions, devoted to the comforting of men's minds, prove the universality of mental suffering. Each of these schools has its place in so far as it is able to relieve suffering, even where it does not eradicate the evil; for with all these schools of healing, the facts of disease and pain remain with us, just as sin and sorrow remain in spite of the many religions.

Disease and pain, like sin and sorrow, are too deep-seated to be removed by palliatives. Our ailments have an ethical cause deeply rooted in the mind. I do not infer by this that physical conditions have no part in disease; they play an import-

ant part as *instruments*, as factors in the chain
of causation. The microbe that carried the black
death was the instrument of uncleanliness, and
uncleanliness is, primarily, a moral disorder. Matter is visible mind, and that bodily conflict which
we call *disease* has a causal affinity to that mental
conflict which is associated with sin. In his present human or self-conscious state, man's mind
is continually being disturbed by violently conflicting desires, and his body attacked by morbid
elements. He is in a state of mental in harmony
and bodily discomfort. Animals in their wild and
primitive state are free from disease because they
are free from inharmony. They are in accord with
their surroundings, have no moral responsibility and no sense of sin, and are free from those
violent disturbances of remorse, grief, disappoint-
ment, etc., which are so destructive of man's
harmony and happiness, and their bodies are
not afflicted. As man ascends into the divine or
cosmic-conscious state, he will leave behind and
below him all these inner conflicts, will overcome
sin and all sense of sin, and will dispel remorse
and sorrow. Being thus restored to mental harmony, he will become restored to bodily harmony,
to wholeness, health.

The body is the image of the mind, and in it are
traced the visible features of hidden thoughts. The

outer obeys the inner, and the enlightened scientist of the future may be able to trace every bodily disorder to its ethical cause in the mentality.

Mental harmony, or moral wholeness, makes for bodily health. I say *makes for it*, for it will not produce it magically, as it were,—as though one should swallow a bottle of medicine and then be whole and free,—but if the mentality is becoming more poised and restful, if the moral stature is increasing, then a sure foundation of bodily wholeness is being laid, the forces are being conserved and are receiving a better direction and adjustment; and even if perfect health is not gained, the bodily derangement, whatever it be, will have lost its power to undermine the strengthened and uplifted mind.

One who suffers in body will not necessarily at once be cured when he begins to fashion his mind on moral and harmonious principles; indeed, for a time, while the body is bringing to a crisis, and throwing off, the effects of former inharmonies, the morbid condition may appear to be intensified. As a man does not gain perfect peace immediately he enters upon the path of righteousness, but must, except in rare instances, pass through a painful period of adjustment; neither does he, with the same rare exceptions, at once acquire perfect health. Time is required for bodily as well as mental readjustment, and even if health is not reached, it will be approached.

If the mind be made robust, the bodily condition will take a secondary and subordinate place, and will cease to have that primary importance which so many give to it. If a disorder is not cured, the mind can rise above it, and refuse to be subdued by it. One can be happy, strong, and useful in spite of it. The statement so often made by health specialists that a useful and happy life is impossible without bodily health is disproved by the fact that numbers of men who have accomplished the greatest works—men of genius and superior talent in all departments—have been afflicted in their bodies, and today there are plenty of living witnesses to this fact. Sometimes the bodily affliction acts as a stimulus to mental activity, and aids rather than hinders its work. To make a useful and happy life dependent upon health, is to put matter before mind, is to subordinate spirit to body.

Men of robust minds do not dwell upon their bodily condition if it be in any way disordered—*they ignore it*, and work on, live on, as though it were not. This ignoring of the body not only keeps the mind sane and strong, but it is the best resource for curing the body. If we cannot have a perfectly sound body, we can have a healthy mind, and a healthy mind is the best route to a sound body.

A sickly mind is more deplorable than a disordered body, and it leads to sickliness of body. The mental invalid is in a far more pitiable condition than the bodily invalid. There are invalids (every physician knows them) who only need to lift themselves into a strong, unselfish, happy frame of mind to discover that their body is whole and capable.

Sickly thoughts about oneself, about one's body and food, should be abolished by all who are called by the name of *man*. The man who imagines that the wholesome food he is eating is going to injure him, needs to come to bodily vigour by the way of mental strength. To regard one's bodily health and safety as being dependent on a particular kind of food which is absent from nearly every household, is to court petty disorders. The vegetarian who says he dare not eat potatoes, that fruit produces indigestion, that apples give him acidity, that pulses are poison, that he is afraid of green vegetables, and so on, is demoralizing the noble cause which he professes to have espoused, is making it look ridiculous in the eyes of those robust meat-eaters who live above such sickly fears and morbid self-scrutinies. To imagine that the fruits of the earth, eaten when one is hungry and in need of food, are destructive of health and life is totally to misunderstand the nature and office of food. The office of food is to sustain and preserve the body, not to undermine and destroy it. It is a strange delusion—and one that must react deleteriously upon the body—that possesses so many who are seeking health by the way of diet, the delusion that certain of the simplest, most natural, and purest of viands are *bad of themselves*, that they have in them the elements of death, and not of life. One of these food-reformers once told me that he believed his ailment (as well as the ailments of thousands of others) was caused by eating bread; not by an excess of bread, but by the bread itself; and yet this man's bread food consisted of nutty, homemade, wholemeal loaves. Let us get rid of our sins, our sickly thoughts, our self-indulgences and foolish excesses before attributing our diseases to such innocent causes.

Dwelling upon one's petty troubles and ail-ments is a manifestation of weakness of character. To so dwell upon them in thought leads to frequent talking about them, and this, in turn, impresses them more vividly upon the mind, which soon becomes demoralized by such petting and pitying. It is as convenient to dwell upon happiness and health as upon misery and disease; as easy to talk about them, and much more pleasant and profit-able to do so.

*Let us live happily then, not hating those who
hate us!*
*Among men who hate us let us dwell free from
hatred!*

*Let us live happily then, free from ailments
among the ailing!*
*Among men who are ailing let us dwell free from
ailments!*

*Let us live happily then, free from greed among
the greedy!*
*Among men who are greedy let us dwell free
from greed!*

Moral principles are the soundest foundations for health, as well as for happiness. They are the true regulators of conduct, and they embrace every detail of life. When earnestly espoused and intelligently understood they will compel a man to reorganize his entire life down to the most apparently insignificant detail. While definitely regulating one's diet, they will put an end to squeamishness, food-fear, and foolish whims and groundless opinions as to the harmfulness of foods. When sound moral health has eradicated self-indulgence and self-pity, all natural foods will be seen as they are—nourishers of the body, and not its destroyers.

Thus a consideration of bodily conditions brings us inevitably back to the mind, and to those moral virtues which fortify it with an invincible protection. The morally right are the bodily right. To be continually transposing the details of life from passing views and fancies, without reference to fixed principles, is to flounder in confusion; but to discipline details by moral principles is to see, with enlightened vision, all details in their proper place and order.

For it is given to moral principles alone, in their personal domain, to perceive the moral order. In them alone resides the insight that penetrates to causes, and with them only is the power to at once command all details to their order and place, as the magnet draws and polarizes the filings of steel.

Better even than curing the body is to rise above it; to be its master, and not to be tyrannized over by it; not to abuse it, not to pander to it, never to put its claims before virtue; to discipline and moderate its pleasures, and not to be overcome by its pains—in a word, to live in the poise and strength of the moral powers, this, better than bodily cure, is yet a safe way to cure, and it is a permanent source of mental vigour and spiritual repose.

Poverty

Many of the greatest men through all ages have abandoned riches and adopted poverty to better enable them to accomplish their lofty purposes. Why, then, is poverty regarded as such a terrible evil? Why is it that this poverty, which these great men regard as a blessing, and adopt as a bride, should be looked upon by the bulk of mankind as a scourge and a plague? The answer is plain. In the one case, the poverty is associated with a nobility of mind which not only takes from it all appearance of evil, but which lifts it up and makes it appear good and beautiful, makes it seem more attractive and more to be desired than riches and honour, so much so that, seeing the dignity and happiness of the noble mendicant, thousands imitate him by adopting his mode of life. In the other case, the poverty of our great cities is associated with everything that is mean and repulsive—with swearing, drunkenness, filth, laziness, dishonesty, and crime. What, then, is the primary evil: is it poverty, or is it sin? The answer is inevitable—it is sin. Remove sin from poverty, and its sting is gone; it has ceased to be the gigantic evil that it appeared, and can even be turned to good and noble ends. Confucius held up one of his poor disciples, Yen-hwui by name, as an example of lofty virtue to his richer pupils, yet "although he was so poor that he had to live on rice and water, and had no better shelter than a hovel, he uttered no complaint. Where this poverty would have made other men discontented and miserable, he did not allow his equanimity to be disturbed." Poverty cannot undermine a noble character, but it can set it off to better advantage. The virtues of Yen-hwui shone all the brighter for being set in poverty, like resplendent jewels set in a contrasting background.

It is common with social reformers to regard poverty as the *cause* of the sins with which it is associated; yet the same reformers refer to the immoralities of the rich as being caused by their riches. Where there is a cause its effect will appear, and were affluence the cause of immorality, and poverty the cause of degradation, then every rich man would become immoral and every poor man would come to degradation.

An evil-doer will commit evil under any circumstances, whether he be rich or poor, or midway between the two conditions. A right-doer will do right howsoever he be placed. Extreme circumstances may help to bring out the evil which is already there awaiting its opportunity, but they cannot cause the evil, cannot create it.

Discontent with one's financial condition is not the same as poverty. Many people regard themselves as poor whose income runs into several hundreds, and in some cases several thousands, of pounds a year, combined with light responsibilities. They imagine their affliction to be poverty; their real trouble is covetousness. They are not made unhappy by poverty, but by the thirst for riches. Poverty is more often in the mind than in the purse. So long as a man thirsts for more money he will regard himself as poor, and in that sense he is poor, for covetousness is poverty of mind. A miser may be a millionaire, but he is as poor as when he was penniless.

On the other hand, the trouble with so many who are living in indigence and degradation is that they *are* satisfied with their condition. To be living in dirt, disorder, laziness, and swinish self-indulgence, revelling in foul thoughts, foul words, and unclean surroundings, and to be satisfied with oneself, is deplorable. Here again, "poverty" resolves itself into a mental condition, and its solution, as a "problem," is to be looked for in the improvement of the individual from within, rather than of his outward condition. Let a man be made clean and alert within, and he will no longer be content with dirt and degradation without. Having put his mind in order, he will then put his house in order; indeed, both he and others will know that he has put himself right by the fact that he has put his immediate surroundings right. His altered heart shows in his altered life.

There are, of course, those who are neither self-deceived nor self-degraded, and yet are poor. Many such are satisfied to remain poor. They are contented, industrious, and happy, and desire nothing else; but those among them who are dissatisfied, and are ambitious for better surroundings and greater scope, should, and usually do, use their poverty as a spur to the exercise of their talents and energies. By self-improvement and attention to duty, they can rise into the fuller, more responsible life which they desire.

Devotion to duty is, indeed, not only the way out of that poverty which is regarded as restrictive, it is also the royal road to affluence, influence, and lasting joy, yea, even to perfection itself. When understood in its deepest sense it is seen to be related to all that is best and noblest in life. It includes energy, industry, concentrated attention to the business of one's life, singleness of purpose, courage and faithfulness, determination and self-reliance, and that self-abnegation which is the key to all real greatness. A singularly successful man was once asked, "What is the secret of your success?" and he replied, "Getting up at six o'clock in the morning, and minding my own business." Success, honour, and influence always come to him who diligently attends to the business of his life, and religiously avoids interfering with the duties of others.

It may here be urged—and is usually so urged—that the majority of those who are in poverty—for instance, the mill and factory workers—have not the time or opportunity to give themselves to any special work. This is a mistake. Time and opportunity are always at hand, are with everybody at all times. Those of the poor above mentioned, who are content to remain where they are, can always be diligent in their factory labour, and sober and happy in their homes, but those of them who feel that they could better fill another sphere, can prepare for it by educating themselves in their spare time. The hard-worked poor are, above all, the people who need to economize their time and energies; and the youth who wishes to rise out of such poverty must at the outset put aside the foolish and wasteful indulgences of alcohol, tobacco, sexual vice, late hours at music-halls, clubs, and gaming parties, and must give his evenings to the improvement of his mind in that course of education which is necessary to his advancement. By this method, numbers of the most influential men throughout history—some of them among the greatest—have raised themselves from the commonest poverty; a fact which proves that the time of necessity is the hour of opportunity, and not, as is so often imagined and declared, the destruction of opportunity; that the deeper the poverty, the greater is the incentive to action in those who are dissatisfied with themselves, and are bent upon achievement.

Poverty is an evil or it is not, according to the character and the condition of mind of the one that is in poverty. Wealth is an evil or not, in the same manner, Tolstoi chafed under his wealthy circumstances. To him they were a great evil. He longed for poverty as the covetous long for wealth. Vice, however, is always an evil, for it both degrades the individual who commits it, and is a menace to society. A logical and profound study of poverty will always bring us back to the individual, and to the human heart. When our social reformers condemn vice as they now condemn the rich;

when they are as eager to abolish wrong-living as they now are to abolish low wages, we may look for a diminution in that form of degraded poverty which is one of the dark spots on our civilization. Before such poverty disappears altogether, the human heart will have undergone, during the process of evolution, a radical change. When that heart is purged from covetousness and selfishness; when drunkenness, impurity, indolence, and self-indulgence are driven for ever from the earth, then poverty and riches will be known no more, and every man will perform his duties with a joy so full and deep as is yet (except to the few whose hearts are already pure) unknown to men, and all will eat of the fruit of their labour in sublime self-respect and perfect peace.

Man's Spiritual Dominion

The kingdom over which man is destined to rule with undisputed sway is that of his own mind and life; but this kingdom, as already shown, is not separate from the universe, is not Confined to itself alone; it is intimately related to entire humanity, to nature, to the current of events in which it is, for the time being, involved, and to the vast universe. Thus the mastery of this kingdom embraces the mastery of the knowledge of life; it lifts a man into the supremacy of wisdom, bestowing upon him the gift of insight into human hearts, giving him the power to distinguish between good and evil, also to comprehend that which is above both good and evil, and to know the nature and consequences of deeds.

At present men are more or less under the sway of rebellious thoughts, and the conquest of these is the supreme conquest of life. The unwise think that everything can be mastered but oneself, and they seek for happiness for themselves and others by modifying external things. The transposing of outward effects cannot bring permanent happiness, or bestow wisdom; the patching and coddling of a sin-laden body cannot produce health and well-being. The wise know that there is no real mastery until self is subdued, that when oneself is conquered, the subjugation of externals is finally assured, and they find happiness for ever springing up within them, in the calm strength of divine virtue. They put away sin, and purify and strengthen the body by rising superior to the sway of its passions.

Man can reign over his own mind; can be lord over himself. Until he does so reign, his life is unsatisfactory and imperfect. His spiritual dominion is the empire of the mental forces of which his nature is composed. The body has no causative power. The ruling of the body—that is, of appetite and passion—is the discipline of mental forces. The subduing, modifying, redirecting, and transmuting of the antagonizing spiritual elements within, is the wonderful and mighty work which all men must, sooner or later, undertake. For a long time man regards himself as the slave of external forces, but there comes a day when his spiritual eyes open, and he sees that he has been a slave this long time to none and nothing but his own ungoverned, unpurified self. In that day, he rises up, and, ascending his spiritual throne, he no longer obeys his desires, appetites, and passions as their slave, but henceforth rules them as his subjects. The mental kingdom through which he has been wont to wander as a puling beggar and a whipped serf, he now discovers is his by right of lordly self-control— his to set in order, to organize and harmonize, to abolish its dissensions and painful contradictions, and bring it to a state of peace.

Thus rising up and exercising his rightful spiritual authority, he enters the company of those kingly ones who in all ages have conquered and attained, who have overcome ignorance, darkness, and mental suffering, and have ascended into Truth.

Conquest: Not Resignation

He who has undertaken the sublime task of overcoming himself, does not resign himself to anything that is evil; he subjects himself only to that which is good. Resignation to evil is the lowest weakness; obedience to good is the highest power. To resign oneself to sin and sorrow, to ignorance and suffering, is to say in effect, "I give up; I am defeated; life is evil, and I submit." Such resignation to evil is the reverse of religion. It is a direct denial of good; it elevates evil to the position of supreme power in the universe. Such submission to evil shows itself in a selfish and sorrowful life; a life alike devoid of strength against temptation, and of that joy and calm which are the manifestation of a mind that is dominated by good.

Man is not framed for perpetual resignation and sorrow, but for final victory and joy. All the spiritual laws of the universe are with the good man, for good preserves and shields. There are no laws of evil. Its nature is destruction and desolation.

The conscious modification of the character away from evil and toward good, forms, at present, no part in the common course of education. Even our religious teachers have lost this knowledge and practice, and cannot, therefore, instruct concerning it. Moral growth is, so far, in the great mass of mankind, unconscious, and is brought about by the stress and struggle of life. The time will come, however, when the conscious formation of character will form an important part in the education of youth, and when no man will be able to fill the position of preacher unless he be a man of habitual self-control, unblemished integrity, and exalted purity, so as to be able to give sound instruction in the making of character, which will then be the main feature of religion.

The doctrine herein set forth by the author is the doctrine of conquest over evil; the annihilation of sin; and necessarily the permanent establishment of man in the knowledge of good, and in the enjoyment of perpetual peace. This is the teaching of the Masters of religion in all ages. Howsoever it may have been disguised and distorted by the unenlightened, it is the doctrine of all the perfect ones that were, and will be the doctrine of all the perfect ones that are to come. It is the doctrine of Truth.

And the conquest is not of an evil without; not of evil men, or evil spirits, or evil things; but of the evil within; of evil thoughts, evil desires, evil deeds; for when every man has destroyed the evil within his own heart, to where in the whole vast universe will any one be able to point, and say, "There is evil"? In that great day when all men have become good within, all traces of evil will have vanished from the earth; sin and sorrow will be unknown; and there will be universal joy for evermore.

Morning *and* Evening Thoughts

Conquer thyself,
Then thou shalt know;
Climb to the high,
Leave thou the low.
Deliverance
Shall him entrance
Who strives with sins and sorrows,
tears and pains.
Till he attains.

–James Allen

First Morning

In aiming at the life of blessedness, one of the simplest beginnings to be considered, and rightly made, is that which we all make every day—namely, the beginning of each day's life. There is a sense in which every day may be regarded as the beginning of a new life, in which one can think, act, and live newly, and in a wiser and better spirit. The right beginning of the day will be followed by cheerfulness permeating the household with a sunny influence, and the tasks and duties of the day will be undertaken in a strong and confident spirit, and the whole day will be well lived.

First Evening

There can be no progress, no achievement, without sacrifice, and a man's worldly success will be in the measure that he sacrifices his confused animal thoughts, and fixes his mind on the development of his plans, and on the strengthening of his resolution and self-reliance. And the higher he lifts his thoughts, the more manly, upright, and righteous he becomes, the greater will be his success, the more blessed and enduring will be his achievements.

Second Morning

None but right acts can follow right thoughts; none but a right life can follow right acts; and by living a right life all blessedness is achieved.

Mind is the Master-power that moulds and makes.
And Man is Mind, and evermore he takes
The Tool of Thought, and, shaping what he wills,
Brings forth a thousand joys, a thousand ills;—
He thinks in secret, and it comes to pass;
Environment is but his looking-glass.

Second Evening

Calmness of mind is one of the beautiful jewels of wisdom. A man becomes calm in the measure that he understands himself as a thought-evolved being . . . and as he develops a right understanding, and sees more and more clearly the internal relations of things by the action of cause and effect, he ceases to fret and fume, and worry and grieve, and remains poised, steadfast, serene.

Third Morning

To follow, under all circumstances, the highest promptings within you; to be always true to the divine self; to rely upon the inward Voice, the inward Light, and to pursue your purpose with a fearless and restful heart, believing that the future will yield unto you the need of every thought and effort; knowing that the laws of the universe can never fail, and that your own will come back to you with mathematical exactitude—this is faith and the living of faith.

Third Evening

Have a thorough understanding of your work, and let it be your own; and as you proceed, ever following the inward Guide, the infallible Voice, you will pass on from victory to victory, and will rise step by step to higher resting-places, and your ever-broadening outlook will gradually reveal to you the essential beauty and purpose of life. Self-purified, health will be yours; self-governed, power will be yours, and all that you do will prosper.

> And I may stand where health, success, and power
> Await my coming, if, each fleeting hour,
> I cling to love and patience; and abide
> With stainlessness; and never step aside
> From high integrity; so shall I see
> At last the land of immortality.

Fourth Morning

When the tongue is well controlled and wisely subdued; when selfish impulses and unworthy thoughts no longer rush to the tongue demanding utterance; when the speech has become harmless, pure, gracious, gentle, and purposeful, and no word is uttered but in sincerity and truth—then are the five steps in virtuous speech accomplished, then is the second great lesson in Truth learned and mastered.

Make pure thy heart, and thou wilt make thy life
Rich, sweet and beautiful.

Fourth Evening

Having clothed himself with humility, the first questions a man asks himself are:—"How am I acting toward others?" "What am I doing to others?" "How am I thinking of others?" "Are my thoughts of, and acts toward, others prompted by unselfish love?" As a man, in the silence of his soul, asks himself these searching questions, he will unerringly see where he has hitherto failed.

Fifth Morning

To dwell in love always and toward all is to live the true life, is to have Life itself. Knowing this, the good man gives up himself unreservedly to the Spirit of Love, and dwells in Love toward all, contending with none, condemning none, but loving all.

The Christ Spirit of Love puts an end, not only to all sin, but to all division and contention.

Fifth Evening

When sin and self are abandoned, the heart is restored to its imperishable Joy.

Joy comes and fills the self-emptied heart; it abides with the peaceful; its reign is with the pure.

Joy flees from the selfish, it deserts the quarrelsome; it is hidden from the impure.

Joy cannot remain with the selfish; it is wedded to Love.

Sixth Morning

In the pure heart there is no room left where personal judgments and hatreds can find lodgment, for it is filled to overflowing with tenderness and love; it sees no evil, and only as men succeed in seeing no evil in others will they become free from sin, and sorrow, and suffering.

> If men only understood
> That the heart that sins must sorrow,
> That the hateful mind tomorrow
> Reaps its barren harvest, weeping,
> Starving, resting not, nor sleeping;
> Tenderness would fill their being,
> They would see with Pity's seeing
> If they only understood.

Sixth Evening

To stand face to face with truth; to arrive, after innumerable wanderings and pains, at wisdom and bliss; not to be finally defeated and cast out, but to ultimately triumph over every inward foe—such is man's divine destiny, such his glorious goal; and this, every saint, sage, and savior has declared.

A man only begins to be a man when he ceases to whine and revile, and commences to search for the hidden justice which regulates his life. And as he adapts his mind to that regulating factor, he ceases to accuse others as the cause of his condition, and builds himself up in strong and noble thoughts; ceases to kick against circumstances; but begins to use them as aids to his more rapid progress, and as a means of discovering the hidden powers and possibilities within himself.

Seventh Morning

The will to evil and the will to good
Are both within thee, which wilt thou employ?
Thou knowest what is right and what is wrong,
Which wilt thou love and foster? which destroy?
Thou art the chooser of thy thoughts and deeds;
Thou art the maker of thine inward state;
The power is thine to be what thou wilt be;
Thou buildest Truth and Love, or lies and hate.

Seventh Evening

The teaching of Jesus brings men back to the simple truth that righteousness, or *right-doing*, is entirely a matter of individual conduct, and not a mystical something apart from a man's thoughts and deeds.

Calmness and patience can become habitual by first grasping, through effort, a calm and patient thought, and then continuously thinking it, and living in it, until "use becomes second nature," and anger and impatience pass away for ever.

Eighth Morning

Man is made or unmade by himself; in the armoury of thought he forges the weapons by which he destroys himself; he also fashions the tools with which he builds for himself heavenly mansions of joy and strength and peace. By the right choice and true application of thought man ascends to the Divine Perfection; by the abuse and wrong application of thought he descends below the level of the beast. Between these two extremes are all the grades of character, and man is their maker and master.

As a being of Power, Intelligence, and Love, and the lord of his own thoughts, man holds the key to every situation.

Eighth Evening

Whatsoever you harbour in the inmost chambers of your heart will, sooner or later, by the inevitable law of reaction, shape itself in your outward life.

Every soul attracts its own, and nothing can possibly come to it that does not belong to it. To realize this is to recognize the universality of Divine Law.

If thou would'st right the world,
And banish all its evils and its woes.
Make its wild places bloom,
And its drear deserts blossom as the rose—
Then right thyself.

Ninth Morning

Whatever conditions are rendering your life burdensome, you may pass out of and beyond them by developing and utilizing within you the transforming power of self-purification and self-conquest.

Before the divine radiance of a pure heart all darkness vanishes and all clouds melt away, and he who has conquered self has conquered the universe.

He who sets his foot firmly upon the path of self-conquest, who walks, aided by the staff of faith, the highway of self-sacrifice, will assuredly achieve the highest prosperity, and will reap abounding and enduring joy and bliss.

Ninth Evening

It is the silent and conquering thought-forces which bring all things into manifestation. The universe grew out of thought.

To adjust all your thoughts to a perfect and unswerving faith in the omnipotence and supremacy of Good, is to co-operate with that Good, and to realize within yourself the solution and destruction of all evil.

To mentally deny evil is not sufficient; it must, by daily practice, be risen above and understood. To affirm the Good mentally is inadequate; it must, by unswerving endeavor, be entered into and comprehended.

Tenth Morning

Every thought you think is a force sent out.

Whatever your position in life may be, before you can hope to enter into any measure of success, usefulness, and power, you must learn how to focus your thought-forces by cultivating calmness and repose.

There is no difficulty, however great, but will yield before a calm and purposeful concentration of thought, and no legitimate object but may be speedily actualized by the intelligent use and direction of one's soul-forces.

Think good thoughts, and they will quickly become actualized in your outward life in the form of good conditions.

Tenth Evening

That which you would be and hope to be, you may be now. Non-accomplishment resides in your perpetual postponement, and, having the power to postpone, you also have the power to accomplish—to perpetually accomplish: Realize this truth, and you shall be today, and every day, the ideal being of whom you dreamed.

Say to yourself, "I will live in my Ideal now; I will manifest my Ideal now; I will be my Ideal now; and all that tempts me away from my Ideal I will not listen to; I will listen only to the voice of my Ideal."

Eleventh Morning

Be as a flower, content to be, to grow in sweetness day by day.

If thou would'st perfect thyself in knowledge, perfect thyself in Love. If thou would'st reach the Highest, ceaselessly cultivate a loving and compassionate heart.

To him who choose Goodness, sacrificing all, is given that which is more than, and includes, all.

Eleventh Evening

The Great Law never cheats any man of his just due.

Human life, when rightly lived, is simple with a beautiful simplicity.

He who comprehends the utter simplicity of life, who obeys its laws, and does not step aside into the dark paths and complex mazes of selfish desire, stands where no harm can reach him.

Then there is fulness of joy, abounding plenty, and rich and complete blessedness.

Twelfth Morning

Every man reaps the results of his own thoughts and deeds, and suffers for his own wrong.

He who begins right, and continues right, does not need to desire and search for felicitous results; they are already at hand; they follow as consequences; they are the certainties, the realities, of life.

Sweet is the rest and deep the bliss of him who has freed his heart from its lusts and hatreds and dark desires.

Twelfth Evening

You are the creator of your own shadows; you desire, and then you grieve; renounce, and then you shall rejoice.

Of all the beautiful truths pertaining to the soul, . . . none is more gladdening or fruitful of divine promise and confidence than this—that man is the master of thought, the moulder of character, and the maker and shaper of character, environment, and destiny.

Thirteenth Morning

As darkness is a passing shadow, and light is substance that remains, so sorrow is fleeting, but joy abides for ever. No true thing can pass away and become lost; no false thing can remain and be preserved. Sorrow is false, and it can not live; Joy is true, and it can not die. Joy may become hidden for a time, but it can always be recovered; sorrow may remain for a period, but it can be transcended and dispersed.

Do not think your sorrow will remain; it will pass away like a cloud. Do not believe that the torments of sin are ever your portion; they will vanish like a hideous nightmare. Awake! Arise! Be holy and joyful.

Thirteenth Evening

Tribulation lasts only so long as there remains some chaff of self which needs to be removed. The *tribulum*, or threshing machine, ceases to work when all the grain is separated from the chaff; and when the last impurities are blown away from the soul, tribulation has completed its work, and there is no more need for it; then abiding joy is realized.

The sole and supreme use of suffering is to purify, to burn out all that is useless and impure. Suffering ceases for him who is pure. There can be no object in burning gold after the dross had been removed.

Fourteenth Morning

In speaking of self-control, one is easily misunderstood. It should not be associated with a destructive repression, but with a constructive expression.

A man is happy, wise and great in the measure that he controls himself; he is wretched, foolish, and mean in the measure that he allows his animal nature to dominate his thoughts and actions.

He who controls himself, controls his life, his circumstances, his destiny; and wherever he goes he carries his happiness with him as an abiding possession.

Renunciation precedes regeneration.

The permanent happiness which men seek in dissipation, excitement, and abandonment to unworthy pleasures, is found only in the life which reverses all this—the life of self-control.

Fourteenth Evening

Law, not confusion, is the dominating principle in the universe; justice, not injustice, is the soul and substance of life; and righteousness, not corruption, is the moulding and moving force in the spiritual government of the world. This being so, man has but to right himself to find that the universe is right.

> When I am pure,
> I shall have solved the mystery of life;
> I shall be sure,
> When I am free from hatred, lust and strife,
> I am in Truth, and Truth abides in me;
> I shall be safe, and sane, and wholly free,
> When I am pure.

Fifteenth Morning

If men only understood.
That their hatred and resentment.
Slays their peace and sweet contentment
Hurts themselves, helps not another,
Does not cheer one lonely brother,
They would seek the better doing
Of good deeds which leaves no rueing—
    If they only understood.

If men only understood
How Love conquers; how prevailing
Is its might, grim hate assailing;
How compassion endeth sorrow,
Maketh wise, and doth not borrow
Pain of passion, they would ever
Live in Love, in hatred never:—
    If they only understood.

Fifteenth Evening

The grace and beauty that were in Jesus can be of no value to you—cannot be understood by you—unless they are also *in you*, and they can never be in you, until you practice them, for, apart from *doing*, the qualities which constitute Goodness do not, as far as you are concerned, exist. To adore Jesus for his good qualities is a long step toward Truth, but to practice those qualities is Truth itself; and he who truly adores the perfection of another will not rest content in his own imperfection, but will fashion his soul after the likeness of that other.

Therefore thou who adorest Jesus for his divine qualities, practice those qualities thyself, and thou too shalt be divine.

Sixteenth Morning

Let a man realize that life in its totality proceeds from the mind, and lo, the way of blessedness is opened up to him! For he will then discover that he possesses the power to rule his mind, and to fashion it in accordance with his Ideal. So will he elect to strongly and steadfastly walk those pathways of thought and action which are altogether excellent; to him life will become beautiful and sacred; and, sooner or later, he will put to flight all evil, confusion, and suffering; for it is impossible for a man to fall short of liberation, enlightenment, and peace, who guards with unwearying diligence the gateway of his heart.

Sixteenth Evening

By constantly overcoming self, a man gains a knowledge of the subtle intricacies of his mind; and it is this divine knowledge which enables him to become established in calmness. Without self-knowledge there can be no abiding peace of mind, and those who are carried away by tempestuous passions, cannot approach the holy place where calmness reigns. The weak man is like one who, having mounted a fiery steed, allows it to run away with him, and carry him whithersoever it wills; the strong main is like one who, having mounted the steed, governs it with a masterly hand, and makes it go in whatever direction and at whatever speed he commands.

Seventeenth Morning

There is no strife, no selfishness, in the Kingdom; there is perfect harmony, equipoise, and rest.

Those who live in the Kingdom of Love, have all their needs supplied by the Law of Love.

As self is the root cause of all strife and suffering, so Love is the root cause of all peace and bliss.

Those who are at rest in the Kingdom, do not look for happiness in any outward possessions. They are freed from all anxiety and trouble, and resting in Love, they are the embodiment of happiness.

Seventeenth Evening

Let it not be supposed that the children of the Kingdom live in ease and indolence (these two sins are the first that have to be eradicated when the search for the Kingdom is entered upon); they live in a peaceful activity; in fact, they only truly live, for the life of self, with its train of worries, griefs, and fears, is not *real life*.

The children of the Kingdom are *known by their life*, they manifest the fruits of the Spirit—"Love, joy, peace, long-suffering, kindness, goodness, faithfulness, meekness, temperance, self-control"—under all circumstances and all vicissitudes.

Eighteenth Morning

The gospel of Jesus is a gospel of *living and doing.* If it were not this it would not voice the Eternal Truth. Its Temple is *Purified Conduct,* the entrance-door to which is *Self-Surrender.* It invites men to shake off sin, and promises, as a result, joy and blessedness and perfect peace.

The Kingdom of Heaven is perfect trust, perfect knowledge, perfect peace. . . . No sin can enter therein, no self-born thought or deed can pass its golden gates; no impure desire can defile its radiant robes. . . . All may enter it who will, but all must pay the price—*the unconditional abandonment of self.*

Eighteenth Evening

I say this—and know it to be truth—*that circumstances can only affect you in so far as you allow them to do so.* You are swayed by circumstances because you have not a right understanding of the nature, use, and power of thought. You believe (and upon this little word *belief* hang all our joys and sorrows) that outward things have the power to make or mar your life; by so doing you submit to those outward things, confess that you are their slave, and they your unconditional master. By so doing you invest them with a power which they do not of themselves possess, and you succumb, in reality not to the circumstances, but to the gloom or gladness, the fear or hope, the strength or weakness, which your thought-sphere has thrown around them.

Nineteenth Morning

If you are one of those who are praying for, and looking forward to, a happier world beyond the grave, here is a message of gladness for you—you may enter into and realize that happy world now; it fills the whole universe, and it is within you, waiting for you to find, acknowledge, and possess. Said one who understood the inner laws of Being— "When men shall say, lo here, or lo there, go not after them. The Kingdom of God is within you."

Nineteenth Evening

Heaven and hell are inward states. Sink into self and all its gratifications, and you sink into hell; rise above self into that state of consciousness which is the utter denial and forgetfulness of self and you enter Heaven.

So long as you persist in selfishly seeking for your own personal happiness, so long will happiness elude you, and you will be sowing the seeds of wretchedness. In so far as you succeed in losing yourself in the service of others, in that measure will happiness come to you, and you will reap a harvest of bliss.

Twentieth Morning

Sympathy given can never be wasted.

One aspect of sympathy is that of pity—pity for the distressed or pain-stricken, with a desire to alleviate or help them in their sufferings. The world needs more of this divine quality.

> For pity makes the world
> Soft to the weak, and noble for the strong.

Another form of sympathy is that of rejoicing with others who are more successful than ourselves, as though their success were our own.

Twentieth Evening

Sweet are companionships, pleasures, and material comforts, but they change and fade away. Sweeter still are Purity, Wisdom, and the knowledge of Truth, and these never change nor fade away.

He who has attained to the possession of spiritual things can never be deprived of his source of happiness; he will never have to part company with it, and wherever he goes in the whole universe, he will carry his possessions with him. His spiritual end will be the fulness of joy.

Twenty–First Morning

Let your heart grow and expand with ever-broadening love, until, freed from all hatred, and passion, and condemnation, it embraces the whole universe with thoughtful tenderness. As the flower opens its petals to receive the morning light, so open your soul more and more to the glorious light of Truth. Soar upward on the wings of aspiration; be fearless, and believe in the loftiest possibilities.

Twenty-First Evening

Mind clothes itself in garments of its own making. Mind is the arbiter of life; it is the creator and shaper of conditions, and the recipient of its own results. It contains within itself both the power to create illusion and to perceive reality.

Mind is the infallible weaver of destiny; thought is the thread, good and evil deeds are the warp and woof; and the web, woven upon the loom of life, is character.

Make pure thy heart, and thou wilt make thy life
Rich, sweet, and beautiful, unmarred by strife.

Twenty-Second Morning

Cherish your visions; cherish your ideals; cherish the music that stirs in your heart, the beauty that forms in your mind, the loveliness that drapes your purest thoughts, for out of them will grow all delightful conditions, all heavenly environment; of these, if you will remain true to them, your world will at last be built.

Guard well thy mind, and, noble, strong, and free,
Nothing shall harm, disturb or conquer thee;
For all thy foes are in thy heart and mind,
There also thy salvation thou shalt find.

Twenty-Second Evening

Dream lofty dreams, and as you dream so shall you become. Your vision is the promise of what you shall one day be; your Ideal is the prophecy of what you shall at last unveil.

The greatest achievement was at first and for a time a dream. The oak sleeps in the acorn; the bird waits in the egg; and in the highest vision of the soul a waking angel stirs.

Your circumstances may be uncongenial, but they shall not long remain so when you perceive an Ideal and strive to reach it.

Twenty-Third Morning

He who has conquered doubt and fear has conquered failure. His every thought is allied with power, and all difficulties are bravely met and wisely overcome. His purposes are seasonably planted, and they bloom and bring forth fruit which does not fell prematurely to the ground.

Thought allied fearlessly to purpose becomes creative force: he who knows this is ready to become something higher and stronger than a mere bundle of wavering thoughts and fluctuating sensations; he who does this has become the conscious and intelligent wielder of his mental powers.

Twenty-Third Evening

Man's true place in the Cosmos is that of a king, not a slave, a commander under the Law of Good, and not a helpless tool in the reign of evil.

I write for men, not for babes; for those who are eager to learn, and earnest to achieve; for those who will put away (for the world's good) a petty personal indulgence, a selfish desire, a mean thought, and live on as though it were not, sans craving and regret.

Man is a master. If he were not, he could not act contrary to law.

Evil and weakness are self destructive.

The universe is girt with goodness and strength, and it protects the good and the strong.

The angry man is the weak man.

Twenty-Fourth Morning

Not by learning will a man triumph over evil; not by much study will he overcome sin and sorrow. Only by conquering himself will he conquer evil; only by practising righteousness will he put an end to sorrow.

Not for the clever, nor the learned, nor the self-confident is the Life Triumphant, but for the pure, the virtuous and wise. The former achieve their particular success in life, but the latter alone achieve the great success so invincible and complete that even in apparent defeat it shines with added victory.

Twenty-Fourth Evening

The true silence is not merely a silent tongue; it is a silent mind. To merely hold one's tongue, and yet to carry about a disturbed and rankling mind, is no remedy for weakness, and no source of power. Silentness, to be powerful, must envelop the whole mind, must permeate every chamber of the heart; it must be the silence of peace. To this broad, deep, abiding silentness a man attains only in the measure that he conquers himself.

Twenty-Fifth Morning

By curbing his tongue, a man gains possession of his mind. The fool babbles, gossips, argues, and bandies words. He glories in the fact that he has had the last word, and has silenced his opponent. He exults in his own folly, is ever on the defensive, and wastes his energies in unprofitable channels. He is like a gardener who continues to dig and plant in unproductive soil.

The wise man avoids idle words, gossip, vain argument, and self-defence. He is content to appear defeated; rejoices when he is defeated; knowing that, having found and removed another error in himself he has thereby become wiser.

Blessed is he who does not strive for the last word.

Desire is *the craving for possession*; aspiration is the *hunger of the heart for peace.* The craving things leads ever farther and farther from peace, and not only ends in deprivation, but is in itself a state of perpetual want. Until it comes to an end, rest and satisfaction are impossible. The hunger for things can never be satisfied, but the hunger for peace can, and the satisfaction of peace is found— is fully possessed, when all selfish desire is abandoned. Then there is fulness of joy, abounding plenty, and rich and complete blessedness.

Twenty-Sixth Morning

A man will reach the Kingdom by purifying himself, and he can only do this by pursuing a process of self-examination and self-analysis. The selfishness must be discovered and understood before it can be removed. It is powerless to remove itself, neither will it pass away of itself. Darkness ceases only when light is introduced; so ignorance can only be dispersed by knowledge, selfishness by love. A man must first of all be willing to lose himself (his self-seeking) before he can find himself (his Divine Self). He must realize that selfishness is not worth clinging to, that it is a master altogether unworthy of his service, and that divine goodness alone is worthy to be enthroned in his heart, as the supreme master of his life.

Twenty-Sixth Evening

Be still my soul, and know that peace is thine.
Be steadfast, heart, and know that strength divine
Belongs to thee; cease from thy turmoil, mind,
And thou the Everlasting Rest shalt find.

If a man would have peace, let him exercise the spirit of peace; if he would find Love, let him dwell in the spirit of Love; if he would escape suffering, let him cease to inflict it; if he would do noble things for humanity, let him cease to do ignoble things for himself. If he will but quarry the mine of his own soul, he shall find there all the materials for building whatsoever he will, and he shall find there also the Central Rock on which to build in safety.

Twenty-Seventh Morning

Men go after much company, and seek out new excitements, but they are not acquainted with peace; in divers paths of pleasure they search for happiness, but they do not come to rest; through diverse ways of laughter and feverish delirium they wander after gladness and life, but their tears are many and grievous, and they do not escape death.

Drifting upon the ocean of life in search of selfish indulgences, men are caught in its storms, and only after many tempests and much privation do they fly to the Rock of Refuge which rests in the deep silence of their own being.

Twenty-Seventh Evening

Meditation centered upon divine realities is the very essence and soul of prayer. It is the silent reaching upward of the soul toward the Eternal.

Meditation is the intense dwelling, in thought, upon an idea or theme with the object of thoroughly comprehending it; and whatsoever you constantly meditate upon, you will not only come to understand, but will grow more and more into its likeness, for it will become incorporated with your very being, will become, in fact, your very self. If, therefore, you constantly dwell upon that which is selfish and debasing, you will ultimately become selfish and debased; if you ceaselessly think upon that which is pure and unselfish, you will surely become pure and unselfish.

Twenty-Eighth Morning

There is no difficulty, however great, but will yield before a calm and powerful concentration of thought, and no legitimate object but may be speedily actualized by the intelligent use and direction of one's soul forces.

Whatever your task may be, concentrate your whole mind upon it; throw into it all the energy of which you are capable. The faultless completion of small tasks leads inevitably to larger tasks. See to it that you rise by steady climbing, and you will never fall.

Twenty-Eighth Evening

He who knows that Love is at the heart of all things, and has realized the all-sufficing power of that Love, has no room in his heart for condemnation.

If you love people, and speak of them with praise, until they in some way thwart you, or do something of which you disapprove, and then you dislike them and speak of them with dispraise, you are not governed by the Love which is of God. If, in your heart, you are continually arraigning and condemning others, selfless love is hidden from you.

Train your mind in strong, impartial, and gentle thought; train your heart in purity and compassion; train your tongue to silence, and to true and stainless speech; so shall you enter the way of holiness and peace, and shall ultimately realize the immortal Love.

Twenty-Ninth Morning

If you would realize true prosperity, do not settle down, as many have done, into the belief that if you do right everything will go wrong. Do not allow the word "competition" to shake your faith in the supremacy of righteousness. I care not what men may say about the "laws of competition," for do not I know the Unchangeable Law which shall one day put them all to rout, and which puts them to rout even now in the heart and life of the righteous man? And knowing this law I can contemplate all dishonesty with undisturbed repose, for I know where certain destruction awaits it.

Under all circumstances do *that which you believe to be right*, and trust the Law; trust the Divine Power which is immanent in the universe, and it will never desert you, and you will always be protected.

Twenty-Ninth Evening

Forget yourself entirely in the sorrows of others, in ministering to others, and divine happiness will emancipate you from all sorrow and suffering. "Taking the first step with a good thought, the second with a good word, and the third with a good deed, I entered Paradise." And you also enter Paradise by pursuing the same course.

Lose yourself in the welfare of others; forget yourself in all that you do—this is the secret of abounding happiness. Ever be on the watch to guard against selfishness, and learn faithfully the divine lessons of inward sacrifice; so shall you climb the highest heights of happiness, and shall remain in the never-clouded sunshine of universal joy, clothed in the shining garment of immortality.

Thirtieth Morning

When the farmer has tilled and dressed his land and put in the seed, he knows that he has done all that he can possibly do, and that now he must trust to the elements, and wait patiently for the course of time to bring about the harvest, and that no amount of expectancy on his part will affect the result. Even so, he who has realized Truth, goes forth as a sower of the seeds of goodness, purity, love, and peace, without expectancy, and never looking for results, knowing that there is the Great Over-ruling Law which brings about its own harvest in due time, and which is alike the source of preservation and destruction.

Thirtieth Evening

The virtuous put a check upon themselves, and set a watch upon their passions and emotions; in this way they gain possession of the mind, and gradually acquire calmness; and as they acquire influence, power, greatness, abiding joy, and fulness and completeness of life.

He only finds peace who conquers himself, who strives, day by day, after greater self-possession, greater self-control, greater calmness of mind.

Where the calm mind is, there is strength and rest, there is love and wisdom; there is one who has fought successfully innumerable battles against self, who, after long toil in secret against his own failings, has triumphed at last.

Thirty-First Morning

Sympathy bestowed increases its store in our own hearts, and enriches and fructifies our own life. Sympathy given is blessedness received; sympathy withheld is blessedness forfeited. In the measure that a man increases and enlarges his sympathy, so much nearer does he approach the ideal life, the perfect blessedness; and when his heart has become so mellowed that no hard, bitter, or cruel thought can enter and detract from its permanent sweetness, then indeed is he richly and divinely blessed.

Thirty-First Evening

Sweet is the rest and deep the bliss of him who has freed his heart from its lusts and hatreds and dark desires; and he who, without any shadow of bitterness resting upon him, and looking out upon the world with boundless compassion and love, can breathe, in his inmost heart, the blessing:

Peace unto all living things,

making no exceptions or distinctions—such a man has reached that happy ending which can never be taken away, for this is the perfection of life, the fulness of peace, the consummation of perfect blessedness.

About the Author

James Allen was one of the pioneering figures of the self-help movement and modern inspirational thought. A philosophical writer and poet, he is best known for his book *As a Man Thinketh*. Writing about complex subjects such as faith, destiny, love, patience, and religion, he had the unique ability to explain them in a way that is simple and easy to comprehend. He often wrote about cause and effect, as well as overcoming sadness, sorrow and grief.

Allen was born in 1864 in Leicester, England into a working-class family. His father travelled alone to America to find work, but was murdered within days of arriving. With the family now facing economic disaster, Allen, at age 15, was forced to leave school and find work to support them.

During stints as a private secretary and stationer, he found that he could showcase his spiritual and social interests in journalism by writing for the magazine *The Herald of the Golden Age*.

In 1901, when he was 37, Allen published his first book, *From Poverty to Power*. In 1902 he began to publish his own spiritual magazine, *The Light of Reason* (which would be retitled *The Epoch* after his death). Each issue contained announcements, an editorial written by Allen on a different subject each month, and many articles, poems, and quotes written by popular authors of the day and even local, unheard of authors.

His third and most famous book *As a Man Thinketh* was published in 1903. The book's minor popularity enabled him to quit his secretarial work and pursue his writing and editing career full time. He wrote 19 books in all, publishing at least one per year while continuing to publish his magazine, until his death. Allen wrote when he had a message—one that he had lived out in his own life and knew that it was good.

In 1905, Allen organized his magazine subscribers into groups (called "The Brotherhood") that would meet regularly and reported on their meetings each month in the magazine. Allen and his wife, Lily Louisa Oram, whom he had married in 1895, would often travel to these group meetings to give speeches and read articles. Some of Allen's favorite writings, and those he quoted often, include the works of Shakespeare, Milton, Emerson, the Bible, Buddha, Whitman, Trine, and Lao-Tze.

Allen died in 1912 at the age of 47. Following his death, Lily, with the help of their daughter, Nora took over the editing of *The Light of Reason*, now under the name *The Epoch*. Lily continued to publish the magazine until her failing eyesight prevented her from doing so. Lily's life was devoted to spreading the works of her husband until her death at age 84.

CPSIA information can be obtained
at www.ICGtesting.com
Printed in the USA
JSHW030001140720
6663JS00001B/54